JN173868

バイリンガルで楽しむ

君野倫子 著

市川染五郎 監修

大島明・マーク 英訳

歌舞伎図鑑

**Photographic Kabuki
Kaleidoscope** in Japanese and English

Written by **KIMINO Rinko**
Supervised by **ICHIKAWA Somegoro**
Translated by Akira Mark OSHIMA

君野倫子 Kimino Rinko

世界の多くの方々に
歌舞伎に出会ってほしい

世界に類を見ない演劇、江戸時代に生まれ長い歴史をもつ歌舞伎の魅力はたくさんありますが、この本を作るにあたって、私にとっての歌舞伎の魅力とは何だろうと、あらためて考えてみました。

一つは今、舞台に立っている役者さん、今、歌舞伎を支えている裏方さんがあるのは、400年もの月日をかけてバトンをつないできた人々がいて、今でも彼らの中にその人々の芸や技が蓄積され息づいているということ。それが他の演劇とは大きく違うところであり、現在もバトンを渡されている過程をお芝居の中に見ることができ、その生き証人になれること、それは大きな魅力の一つです。同じ演目が何千回も上演されても飽きることなく感動できるのは、「人がつないでいる」深みや厚みゆえだと思うのです。

もう一つは、想像でしかわからなかった遠い時代の人々の姿、生活、風俗風習、価値観をいきいきと肌で感じ、その時代の人たちが、このお芝居を観て、何を思い、何を感じたのだろう……と思いをはせることができること。まだ歌舞伎を見始めた頃、そうか江戸時代の人も、もしかすると同じものを観ていたのかもしれない、と気付いたとき、思わず今に歌舞伎を伝えてくださったすべての人に感謝したいと思ったことを、今でもはっきり思い出します。このように歴史あるものを大切に守り伝えてきたのですが、一方で現在も新しい歌舞伎が生まれています。今、生まれている歌舞伎が100年後には古典になっているかもしれないと思うと、また遠く未来にまで思いをはせることができるのも歌舞伎ならではです。

そして日本人の美意識。　無駄なところはそぎ落とされた「型」に見る美しさ。たとえ古典と呼ばれるものであっても、現代の私たちが見ても決して古さを感じさせない色彩やデザインの斬新さ。日本人だけでなく、世界の多くの方々に、この美しいものを創り出す人々の誇り高い姿、歌舞伎に出会ってほしい、そう願ってやみません。この本が、歌舞伎と世界を結ぶ架け橋になれたら幸せです。

I want as many people as possible
from all over the world
to have their own encounter with kabuki.

Born in the Edo period (1603-1868), kabuki is a kind of theater unlike any other in the world. Before I could create this bilingual book, I had to go back and try to remember as clearly as possible just what makes kabuki so special to me.

The first big difference with other world theater is that not only the actors, but the technical staff can only do their work because of a heritage of wisdom, art and techniques that have been painstakingly developed over the 400 years of kabuki's history. All the people of kabuki are living testimony to the fact that they have received the legacy of the past and have made it their own. Probably it is the careful attention to countless details of performance that makes it possible for a classical play to be performed over a thousand times without people ever tiring of it.

Another thing is that kabuki is a kind of time capsule that shows us very concretely how the people of the Edo period (1603 – 1868) lived and looked like and what they believed. Things we could otherwise only guess at are right before our eyes. Once, when I was just starting to watch kabuki, I happened to realize that people in the Edo period probably saw almost the same thing as I was. I remember very clearly that all in a rush, I was overwhelmed with gratitude to all those generations of actors and craftsmen who worked so hard to continue kabuki for those hundreds of years. Then, my mind raced from the distant past to the distant future. Today, at the same time that the people of kabuki treasure their heritage, they also create new kabuki, and in time, some of the things they make may become classics as well.

Then also, kabuki embodies one form of the Japanese aesthetic sense. What seems full of excess and flamboyance is actually a carefully calculated "*kata* (set form)" in which everything unnecessary has been ruthlessly pared away. That is why kabuki may be called a "classical" art form, but doesn't feel old at all. It has colors and designs that seem shockingly fresh and modern even to us today. Japan should be proud of the people of kabuki that have created such a world of beauty and I dearly want as many people as possible – not just Japanese – people all over the world, to be able to have their own encounter with kabuki. If this book contributes to this in even a small way to serve as a bridge between kabuki and the world, I will be very happy.

市川染五郎 Ichikawa Somegoro

興味を引く"何か"が絶対にある

歌舞伎の世界にようこそ！　市川染五郎です。
皆様は歌舞伎をどのようにイメージされているのでしょうか。

歌舞伎をご覧になったことがある方は、イメージをお持ちだとは思いますが、もしかしたら、歌舞伎未体験の方も歌舞伎のイメージをお持ちなのではないでしょうか。それは、歌舞伎が何にも置き換えることのできない極めて日本独自の芸能だからだと思います。例えば、白塗り、隈取、見得、女形、絢爛豪華な色使い、音楽を伴う様式的な演技術……。

どれも他の芸能にはない事柄ばかりです。歌舞伎は400年以上の歴史ある伝統芸能でありながら、時代の流行を敏感に感じてそれを貪欲に取り込み、歌舞伎の新たな息吹となって進化し"エンターテインメント"として現在も生き続けています。ストーリー、仕掛け、化粧、音楽、道具など、芝居を作るあらゆる分野で極められた職人の集合体である歌舞伎の見方は無限にあります。

ストーリーを楽しむことはもちろんですが、それ以外にも楽しみはあります。大道具、衣裳、化粧などの色とその色の組み合わせを楽しむ。鼓、太鼓、三味線という邦楽器、そして人の発する抑揚のある声を含めた歌舞伎音楽を楽しむ。男が創造し、男でしかできない女、女形の艶やかさを楽しむ。出雲阿国という女性が祖である歌舞伎が男性のみで演じるようになった歌舞伎史を楽しむ。何かにフォーカスを合わせて見ていただくと、必ずや興味を引く"何か"があります。

いかがでしょうか。ファンタジーの世界・歌舞伎に"何か"を探しに行きませんか。それを探し当てるのは、読者の皆様お一人おひとりです。そしてこの本が、"何か"を見つけるためのヒント、あるいは足がかりになって深く深く皆様を歌舞伎の世界に誘ってまいります。

さあ、まいりましょう！

Kabuki is infinite: there's something for everybody!

Welcome to the world of kabuki! I'm kabuki actor Ichikawa Somegoro.
What kind of image do you have of kabuki?

Of course, if you've seen kabuki, you have a clear image, but even if you've never actually seen kabuki, I imagine you still have some kind of image. That is probably because kabuki is full of unique, memorable features. For example, there is the *oshiroi* white make-up, the florid red lines of *kumadori* make-up, the *mie* poses, the *onnagata* female role specialists, the brilliant color combinations and the stylized musical acting.

They are in kabuki and nowhere else. Kabuki is a traditional art form with a history of 400 years, but it is very sensitive to its time and quickly incorporates anything that will delight the audience to bring new vigor. It has survived to this day by being a form of entertainment that is constantly evolving. Kabuki is created by craftsmen in all fields – writing, stage devices, make-up, music, stage sets – and all these craftsmen have perfected their craft. This means there are an infinite number of ways to enjoy kabuki.

You can enjoy kabuki's stories as drama, of course, but there are all kinds of other ways to appreciate kabuki. You can look at the stunning colors and color combinations of the sets, costumes and make-up. You can enjoy the music created by Japanese musical instruments like the *tsuzumi* hand drum, the *taiko* stick drum and the three-stringed *shamisen*. And then, you can listen to the interplay between the instrumental music and the musical way that the actors speak their lines. Also, you can focus on the unique art of the *onnagata* female role specialist, a femininity imagined by men and that can only be performed by men. Or you can reflect on the strange twists of kabuki's history; that an art form created by a woman named Izumo no Okuni is now performed entirely by men. No matter what aspect of kabuki you focus on, there will be something to draw you in.

So how about it? Are you ready to start exploring the world of kabuki and find that something that is waiting for you? The search is different for everyone. This book can provide some hints, or maybe it will provide a series of footholds that will draw you deeper and deeper into the world of kabuki.

Let's begin the journey!

目次　Contents

はじめに　君野倫子 ·· 2
Foreword　Kimino Rinko

はじめに　市川染五郎 ·· 4
Foreword　Ichikawa Somegoro

女形の世界　The World of *Onnagata* Female Roles

歌舞伎では姫から老婆まで、女性の役も男性の役者が
演じます。これを「女形」といいます。花魁の圧倒的な
美しさ、近くでじっくり見てみたいと思った色鮮やかな
衣裳の数々、かわいらしい髪飾りや特徴的な鬘、江戸時
代の女性の身だしなみなど、女形ならではの美しさを楽
しんでください。

In kabuki, all female roles, from beautiful princesses to old women, are played by male actors
called "*onnagata*." This chapter introduces the
unique world of the *onnagata*, from beautifully
colored costumes, hair ornaments and wigs to all
the cosmetics and accessories that women in the
Edo period used to make themselves beautiful.

情熱を表す姫様の赤 ··· 12
Red Shows a Princess's Passionate Heart

豊かさの象徴　見事な友禅 ·· 14
Multi-Colored *Yuzen* Dyeing: A Symbol of Wealth

春風を思わせる日本の色 ·· 15
Japanese Color Sense: Colors Like a Spring Breeze

豪華絢爛　花魁道中 ··· 16
Gorgeous Costumes for a Courtesan on Parade

凛と気高き　お座敷の花魁 ·· 18
A Courtesan's Splendid Pride in the Banquet Room

真紅の色無地　女の信念 ·· 20
Pure Unpatterned Red Shows a Principled Woman

舞台に映える色合わせ …………………………………… 22
Colors Come to Life on Stage

化身を表す伝統文様 ……………………………………… 24
Traditional Motifs Show Monstrous Transformations

色っぽい芸者の着こなし ………………………………… 25
The Subtle Sensual Touches of a Geisha's Kimono

身分がわかる帯結び ……………………………………… 26
The Style of *Obi* Knot Shows Social Position

垣間見る江戸の化粧 ……………………………………… 28
A Glimpse of Edo Period Make-Up

　◆江戸時代の携帯化粧道具 …………………………… 29
　　Edo Period Portable Make-Up Tools

女形の鬘と髪飾り …………………………………………… 30
Onnagata Wigs and Hair Ornaments

意味持つ女のかぶり物 …………………………………… 34
Female Headgear with Special Meanings

立役の世界　The World of *Tachiyaku* Male Roles

　「女形」に対し、男性の役を「立役」といいます。長く愛されてきた歌舞伎の代表的な立役、役の想いや性格をよく表した衣裳の色使い、武士を象徴する裃や長袴、役の数だけあるといわれる鬘、受け継がれてきた先駆者への想いまで感じてください。

　Actors who play male roles are called *"tachiyaku."* This chapter introduces some of the popular male roles of kabuki, the thoughts and emotions that go into costumes, the ceremonial crested *kamishimo* formal wear of samurai and long *nagabakama* trousers, wigs as numerous as male roles and designs that recall famous actors of the past.

忠義のヒーロー　山伏スタイル ………………………… 36
A *Yamabushi* Mountain Priest: A Loyal Hero

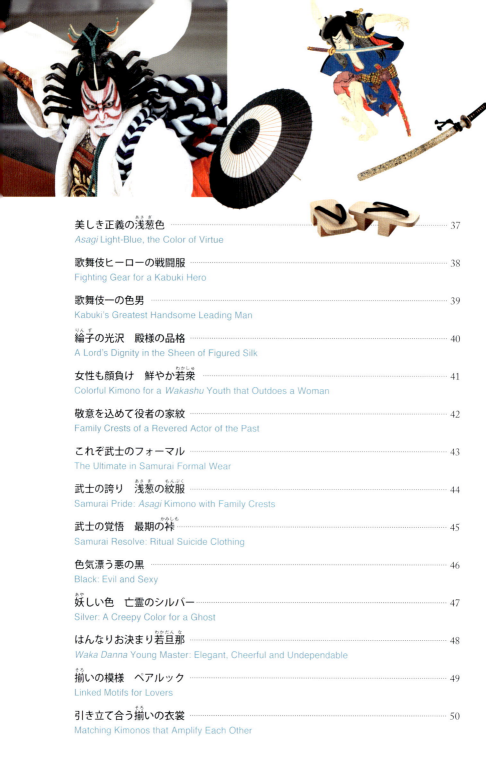

美しき正義の浅葱色 37
Asagi Light-Blue, the Color of Virtue

歌舞伎ヒーローの戦闘服 38
Fighting Gear for a Kabuki Hero

歌舞伎一の色男 39
Kabuki's Greatest Handsome Leading Man

綸子の光沢　殿様の品格 40
A Lord's Dignity in the Sheen of Figured Silk

女性も顔負け　鮮やか若衆 41
Colorful Kimono for a *Wakashu* Youth that Outdoes a Woman

敬意を込めて役者の家紋 42
Family Crests of a Revered Actor of the Past

これぞ武士のフォーマル 43
The Ultimate in Samurai Formal Wear

武士の誇り　浅葱の紋服 44
Samurai Pride: *Asagi* Kimono with Family Crests

武士の覚悟　最期の裃 45
Samurai Resolve: Ritual Suicide Clothing

色気漂う悪の黒 46
Black: Evil and Sexy

妖しい色　亡霊のシルバー 47
Silver: A Creepy Color for a Ghost

はんなりお決まり若旦那 48
Waka Danna Young Master: Elegant, Cheerful and Undependable

揃いの模様　ペアルック 49
Linked Motifs for Lovers

引き立て合う揃いの衣裳 50
Matching Kimonos that Amplify Each Other

名前そのまま着物の文様 ································· 52
Role Names that Become Patterns

誰もが大きくなれる肉襦袢 ························· 54
Niku-Juban Flesh Costume: Anyone Can Become a Muscleman

江戸の男のちらリズム ······························· 55
The Pride of an Edo Man Peeks Out

鬘でわかる立役の身分 ···························· 56
Wigs for *Tachiyaku* Roles of Different Status

番外編 役に応じた　カラフル足袋 ················· 60
Extra Colorful *Tabi* for All Kinds of Different Roles

小道具　Hand Props

　役者が手にする小道具は、たとえ、小さくて客席から見えなくても、一つひとつ、その場、その役にふさわしいものが用意されています。そのディテールやこだわりをじっくり見てください。

　The various hand props are all carefully made to create a feeling of reality and the character. Even if it is something very small that can't be seen well by the audience, each one has been prepared with careful attention to detail.

食べ物 ···················· 62
Food

十手・刀 ················· 66
Jitte and Swords

扇 ·························· 68
Ogi (fans)

履物 ······················ 72
Footwear

年中行事 ···················· 64
Seasonal Ceremonies

吹雪 ························· 67
Fubuki (paper snow and flower petals)

傘 ···························· 70
Paper Umbrellas

手ぬぐい ···················· 74
Tenugui (handcloths)

のれん 76
Noren (split curtains)

楽器 78
Musical Instruments

文房具 80
Stationary Items

髪結道具 81
Hairdressing Tools

動物 82
Animals

キセル 86
Kiseru (tobacco pipes)

◆小道具を使った演じ分け 87
Using the Props Differently for Different Role Types

歌舞伎の特徴　Unique Features of Kabuki

　歌舞伎には歌舞伎にしか見られない独特の化粧法、約束事、演出方法などがあります。それを知っておくだけでも歌舞伎を観る楽しみが倍増します。

　There are all kinds of conventions, special make-ups and other features unique to kabuki. Just knowing a little about these things can make viewing kabuki more enjoyable.

隈取 88
Kumadori Make-Up

黒衣 92
Kurogo (assistants in black)

ぶっかえり 96
Bukkaeri Fast Costume Change

屋号と共に受け継ぐ家紋 98
Crests Inherited Together with Yago House Names

個性を競う役者の文様 100
Highly Individual Patterns with Actors' Names

こしらえ 90
Koshirae (preparations)

引き抜き 94
Hikinuki Fast Costume Change

歌舞伎舞台を支える人達 Indispensable Kabuki Staff

歌舞伎は役者さんだけでは語れません。まさにあらゆる面で、役者さんを陰で支えるプロ集団がいるのです。各裏方さんの想い、仕事の流れ、受け継がれてきた技術などをご紹介します。

Kabuki is not just the actors. Kabuki is supported by large numbers of skilled artists and craftsmen. This chapter will look at the various groups of stage staff and their skills that make kabuki possible.

黒御簾音楽 ···································· 102
Kuro-misu Background Music

女形の床山 ···································· 106
Tokoyama (wig dresser) for Onnagata

鬘屋 ···································· 110
Katsura-ya (wig maker)

大道具 ···································· 114
Odogu (stage set crew)

衣裳 ···································· 104
Isho (costumers)

立役の床山 ···································· 108
Tokoyama (wig dresser) for Tachiyaku

小道具 ···································· 112
Kodogu (props)

本書に登場する演目のバイリンガルリスト ···································· 118
Bilingual List of Plays Mentioned in the Text

チケットを買うには ···································· 120
How to Buy Kabuki Tickets

歌舞伎を楽しめる劇場リスト ···································· 121
Theaters Performing Kabuki Regularly

歌舞伎の舞台 ···································· 122
Parts of the Kabuki Stage

おわりに　市川染五郎 ···································· 124
Afterword　Ichikawa Somegoro

おわりに　君野倫子 ···································· 126
Afterword　Kimino Rinko

本文中の『　』は演目名、《　》は通称、〈　〉は場面を表す。

情熱を表す姫様の赤

金糸、銀糸の刺しゅうで四季折々の花、霞や雲がほどこされた赤い振袖は、高貴で華やかで美しい武家の姫様の衣裳。一途で情熱の赤です。歌舞伎の姫役が赤い着物を着ていることが多いので、お姫様の役柄を総称して「赤姫」と呼びます。姫は世間知らずで純情可憐、なのに思い込んだら命がけの一途さ。姫は姫だわ……と思いつつ、憎めないかわいらしさ。まさに衣裳の赤に情熱が象徴されているようです。姫を演じる役者は、華やかさと気品を兼ね備えていなければなりません。

The red kimono with flowing sleeves shows the elegance and beauty of a princess from a high-ranking samurai family. It is embroidered with flowers of the four seasons, clouds and bands of mist lavish use of gold and silver thread. Sometimes there are other colored kimonos, but this color is so common that they are called "*akahime* (red princesses)". Red shows the unwavering passion of a princess when she finds her true love. A princess is delicate and sheltered, but when she falls in love, she is unstoppable and will even risk her life for the sake of her love. The actor must have elegance and beauty to match this role type.

赤姫はどの姫もほぼ同じ髪形、髪飾り。キラキラの前ざしの素材は紙です。
Princesses all have the same hair styles and ornaments. The ornamental tiara is made of paper.

房付きの扇子と美しい袋に入った懐剣が姫の必需品。
Princesses all have fans with tassels and daggers in beautiful bags.

13

豊かさの象徴　見事な友禅

Multi-Colored *Yuzen* Dyeing: A Symbol of Wealth

『新版歌祭文』のお染は大坂の油屋のお嬢様。かわいい友禅染の振袖に縮子の黒と鹿子絞りの麻の葉模様の帯。発色の素晴らしさ、ひときわ色鮮やかな着物が華やかで舞台照明に映えます。帯はだらりに結ぶのがお嬢様のトレードマークです。

Osome in "*Shinpan Uta Zaimon*" is the daughter of the wealthy Aburaya in Osaka. She has a delicate *yuzen* dyed kimono with long sleeves with an *obi* of cloth *shibori* dyed in a dappled pattern of a starburst of leaves and lined with black satin. The *obi* hangs down very long: a sign this is a girl from a good family.

『春興鏡獅子』の前半に登場する可憐な
御小姓、弥生の衣裳は、上品で春を感じさ
せるような繊細な色です。歌舞伎の衣裳に
は、四季の微妙な移ろいを感じさせる日本
独特の色彩や美意識が表れていて、配色の
妙も見事です。

Yayoi is a young girl serving in the
shogun's court who appears in the first
half of "Kagami Jishi." The elegant colors
delicately suggest spring. Many of the
colors of kabuki costumes express the
finest changes in the seasons with great
subtlety.

豪華絢爛　花魁道中

Gorgeous Costumes for a Courtesan on Parade

江戸時代、公許の三大遊廓といえば、江戸吉原、京都島原、大坂新町でした。何千人もの遊女の中で花魁になれたのはほんの数人だったそう。もちろん、道中できるのは花魁のみ。花魁道中は前から順に箱提灯を持った若い衆、遊女見習い、奉公に来たばかりの幼い禿、そして少し年配のマネージャーのような存在が数人で総勢約10名が歩きました。

花魁は遊里一の教養と美貌を兼ね備えた遊女なので、歌舞伎の中で演じる役者さんにも、その衣裳の豪華さ、華やかさに負けない存在感が必要になります。鬘、衣裳合わせて30kg!!　道中が花道をすすみ、花魁が客席に向かい言葉を発する瞬間、その美しさに男性が演じていることを忘れてしまいます。現代では、こんな豪華な花魁を生で見られるのは歌舞伎だけでしょう。

In the Edo period, the three great licensed brothel districts were Yoshiwara in Edo, Shimabara in Kyoto and Shinmachi in Osaka. Out of the thousands of prostitutes there, only a very few reached the exalted rank of *oiran*. The *oiran* had grand processions through the quarter with nearly a dozen people including child apprentices, younger courtesans and other attendants.

The kabuki actors playing *oiran* must have a presence that projects over the lavish costumes. The wig and costume combined can be 30 kg. This sight only remains in kabuki and when the *oiran* steps out onto the *hanamichi* runway, it is so breathtaking, you forget that she is played by a man.

道中着
Procession Kimono

光沢のある繻子地に鳳凰と桐の刺しゅうたっぷりの裲襠。裾にはたっぷり綿が入っていて、さらに豪華です。

There is an embroidered phoenix and paulownia leaves on a shiny satin base with storm clouds on the padded hem.

下駄
Wooden Clogs

道中で履く高さ20cm 以上、重さ 3 kg もある桐の黒塗りの三歯下駄。

She wore black wooden clogs with three supports. They were over 20 cm. high and weighed 3 kg.

『助六由縁江戸桜』揚巻（坂東玉三郎）　*Sukeroku Yukari no Edo Zakura*, Agemaki (Bando Tamasaburo)

凜と気高き　お座敷の花魁

A Courtesan's Splendid Pride in the Banquet Room

花魁は座敷で客より上座に座ります。金さえ払えば、いきなり花魁と床をともにできるわけではありません。1度目は遠くから見るだけ、2回目は挨拶とお話だけ、3回目は花魁が了解すれば、初めて床入れがかなったといいます。初会だけ一両一分。禿時代から三味線、琴、茶道など、花魁になるべく英才教育されます。

The *oiran* were remote and fabulously expensive. There was no talk the first meeting, the second time there were only a few formal greetings. It took three meetings, each with the fees for a banquet, before a patron could actually sleep with her, but even then, only if the *oiran* agreed. They had to be refined and cultured and from the time they were child apprentices they would learn *shamisen*, *koto*, tea ceremony and other elegant pursuits.

座敷用の着物の掛け衿の部分は取り外しができるように、しつけ糸で留めてあります。衿をはずすことで、自分の身を削ってまで「あなたに尽くします」という気持ちを表しています。
The collar of the kimono is held on with basting threads so that it can be taken off at any time. Removing the collar suggests that the courtesan is willing to sacrifice parts of her self to serve her man.

『籠釣瓶花街酔醒』八ツ橋(尾上菊之助)
Kagotsurube Sato no Eizame, Yatsuhashi (Onoe Kikunosuke)

「今様押絵鏡　芸者長吉」
歌川豊国(三代)画・安政 6(1859)年
"Geisha Chokichi"
by Utagawa Toyokuni Ⅲ (1859).

「今様押絵鏡　七綾太夫」
歌川豊国（三代）画・安政6（1859）年
"Nana-Ayatayu" by Utagawa Toyokuni Ⅲ (1859).

お座敷着　**Formal Reception Kimono**
お座敷には同じ柄の着物を重ねて着ます。上に着る着物（写真右）を脱ぐと花魁の普段着（写真上）になります。
The overrobe (right) and kimono (above) have matching patterns, but the top half of the kimono is underkimono material. So when she took off her overrobe, she was already half in her underwear.

　歌舞伎には、若い町人が花魁に惚れて金をつぎこみ、身請けする、しないで最後は殺しか心中かという芝居があります。江戸時代に実際に起きた事件をもとに書かれたものです。華やかなイメージの花魁ですが、所詮は遊女。あの重い衣裳に高さ20cm以上もある履物。決して吉原から逃げられない悲しい人生なのです。

There are many kabuki plays where the money spent on a courtesan leads to tragedy. Many of these plays are based on real incidents. No matter how fabulous the *oiran*, she was still a prostitute and the heavy costume and tall *geta* clogs (over 20 cm) were to make sure she could not run away.

19

真紅の色無地　女の信念

Pure Unpatterned Red Shows a Principled Woman

1人の役者が十役演じる、通称
《伊達の十役》のこの作品にも
政岡が登場する。
Masaoka in "The Ten Roles
of Sendai Hagi," a version of
the play with one actor playing ten roles.

『慙紅葉汗顔見勢』政岡（市川染五郎）　*Haji Momiji Ase no Kaomise*, Masaoka (Ichikawa Somegoro)

『伽羅先代萩』の政岡は、幼君の身代わりになっ
て死んだ我が子と２人きりになったとき、補襠
を脱ぎ、息子にかけ、抱きかかえて涙します。
補襠を脱いだ瞬間、目に飛び込んでくる真紅の

色無地。女性・母親であることを超えて、果た
さねばならない忠義。その信念と忠誠心、女の
強さを衣裳に表しています。この計算しつくさ
れた衣裳に負けない役者さんにも注目です。

In "*Meiboku Sendai Hagi* (The Troubles in the Date Clan)," Masaoka is nurse to the young
lord and even sacrifices her own child to protect him. Masaoka performs her duty unwaver-
ingly until the lord is safe and she is with the dead body of her child. She covers the body with
the black overrobe that is the symbol of her office and exposes her red kimono. The flash of red
shows the principles by which she lives, which must come before her feelings as a mother. The
actor must be able to express all the aspects of this subtle and carefully calculated costume.

『伽羅先代萩』の政岡は、女形最高の大役
の一つといわれています。
Masaoka is considered one of the most
difficult roles for an *onnagata*.

伊達家の家紋である竹と雀が刺しゅうされた裲襠。政岡の忠
誠心を表しています。
The design combines the sparrows and bamboo of the
crest of the Date clan with snow, expressing the way
Masaoka remains loyal under unbearable pressure.

舞台に映える色合わせ

Colors Come to Life on Stage

歌舞伎らしさを象徴するような衣裳の色合わせに出会うとハッとさせられます。衣裳は照明が当たったときにどんな色に見えるかを考えて染められるそう。ストーリーや歌舞伎の約束事がわからなくても、まずは大胆な色彩美をご堪能いただきたいです。

The color combinations of kabuki are truly breathtaking. Fabrics are dyed with an eye to what the colors will look like under stage lights. Even without knowing the stories or the traditional conventions of kabuki, you can feel the boldness of the colors of kabuki.

『妹背山婦女庭訓』に登場する田舎の娘・お三輪の衣裳。美しい萌葱色を基調に十六武蔵という江戸時代に流行したボードゲームの柄を配した、遊び心ある着物です。歩くたびに見える裾まわしの赤が印象的です。

The costume for the country girl Omiwa in "*Imoseyama Onna Teikin*" has a green background, and a board game. Each step reveals a glimpse of the bright red bottom hem.

お三輪をはじめとして若い娘が着る、麻の葉段鹿子柄の長襦袢。鹿子絞りの点で描かれた麻の葉模様が緋色と浅葱色で段々に描かれていることから「段鹿子」と呼びます。舞台上で見るこの配色は、実に美しく色鮮やかです。

This is the under kimono that young girls like Omiwa wear. The design is called "*asanoha dan kanoko*" because a dappled tie-dye pattern of flax leaves in scarlet and light blue is arranged in diagonal stripes.

「東海道五十三次の内　鳴海／人丸」
歌川豊国(三代)画・嘉永5(1852)年
"Hitomaru" by Utagawa Toyokuni Ⅲ (1852)

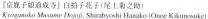

『京鹿子娘道成寺』白拍子花子（尾上菊之助）
Kyoganoko Musume Dojoji, Shirabyoshi Hanako (Onoe Kikunosuke)

『京鹿子娘道成寺』に登場する白拍子花子の衣裳は、三角形を連続させた柄で、魚や蛇のうろこを想像させるうろこ文。病魔や悪霊から身を守る厄除け柄として親しまれてきた古来日本に伝わる文様です。歌舞伎では鬼女や蛇の化身、魔性を表す衣裳として使われ、老婆や美しい姫が実は……と、正体を現す場面などに見られます。役者の表情の変化も見逃せません。

This costume from "*Musume Dojoji* (The Girl at Dojoji Temple)" has a pattern of triangles that suggest the scales of a fish or serpent. This pattern was used in ancient times to ward off illness and evil spirits. In kabuki it is used to suggest that a character is a demoness or a serpent. This is the pattern that is used when their true nature is revealed. That sweet old lady or beautiful princess might be a monster! Don't miss the expression on the actor's face at the moment of transformation.

色っぽい芸者の着こなし

The Subtle Sensual Touches of a Geisha's Kimono

『お祭り』芸者（坂東玉三郎）
Omatsuri, Geisha (Bando Tamasaburo)

　「芸者」は文字通り、お座敷で三味線を弾いたり、義太夫を語ったり、踊ったりする「芸を見せる」プロです。色を売る「遊女」とは、まったく違うものでした。黒の着物に白献上の帯、赤の帯揚げの粋ないでたち、衿（えり）の出し具合、衿合わせの角度、帯のずらし方、赤の帯揚げの出し方、芸者独特の色気のある着付け方です。役者の芸者ならではの立ち振る舞いにも注目です。

　The word "geisha" means "an artist," in this case, a performing artist, and geisha perform music and dances in the banquet chamber. They were never prostitutes like the courtesans were. Their costume is subdued, but chic: a black silk kimono, white *kenjo obi* and red *obi-age* sash to set off the *obi*. Little touches make the costume distinctive: how much the collar of the under-kimono shows, how much of the red of the sash shows – these make the feeling of the geisha's costume unique.

帯を見ていると、時代や身分によって帯の素材や結び方が違うのがわかります。

The material and way the obi is tied differs depending on the period setting of the play and the social position of the character.

画題不明　歌川豊国(三代)・安政5(1858)年
Woodblock print by Utagawa Toyokuni III (1858)

矢の字
Ya no Ji ("Arrowhead")

腰元、御殿女中が結んでいる黒繻子の帯。背中にぴたりとついて動きやすく、外出するときは羽根が左上に、屋内では右上になるように結ぶのが一般的。

This black satin silk *obi* is tied in the style of maids serving in samurai mansions. It is flat against the back for easy movement. When going out, the upper tip of the knot is on the left; inside the mansion, it is to the right.

だらり
Darari ("Hanging loose")

姫や若い娘が結ぶ長く垂れ下がった結び方。
The knot for young women from good families.

文庫
Bunko ("Box")

武家文庫ともいわれ、武家の女房、奥女中の局などが裲襠の下に結んでいます。江戸中期に生まれた結び方。
This style is also called "*buke bunko* (samurai box)." This is the way the *obi* is tied under the overrobes of the wives of samurai and high-ranking ladies-in-waiting.

まないた
Manaita ("Cutting board")
花魁が道中で締める帯を「まないた帯」と呼び、その刺しゅうや織りの華やかさには圧倒されます。

This is the *obi* for a top-ranking courtesan on parade. The big flap in front is like a cutting board and is covered with woven and embroidered designs.

柳
Yanagi ("Willow")
帯締めがほどけてはらりと落ちたお太鼓が、柳のように揺れて色っぽいとその名がついたとか。手先は体の前帯にはさみます。芸者が締めています。

Instead of tying the back in a loop, it hangs loose, suggesting the branches of a willow tree. The end of the *obi* is tucked into the front. This is the style for geisha.

ひっかけ
Hikkake ("Tucking in")
長屋の女房や年寄りがしていますが、手元を見ないでも結べる簡単さにびっくり！

This is a style for commoner women living in tenements or older women. It's so simple you can do it without looking.

角出し
Tsuno-dashi ("Horns sticking out")
歌舞伎ではよく商家や長屋の女房が結びます。ふっくらと形よく、本当にかっこいいです。

In kabuki this is often used for merchant wives and other commoners. It has a nice rounded form and looks great!

垣間見る江戸の化粧

A Glimpse of Edo Period Make-Up

『与話情浮名横櫛』のお富がお湯帰りに赤い糠袋をくわえて帰ってくる場面があります。江戸時代、女性が銭湯へ行くときは糠袋を欠かさず持っていき、お湯につけて絞った白い汁を石けん代わりにしました。こうした江戸時代の女性の風習や習慣に加え、歌舞伎の中で女性が髪を整え、化粧する色っぽい様子や道具なども現代とは違って興味深いです。

In *"Kirare Yosa (Scarfaced Yosaburo),"* there is the sensuous sight of Otomi returning from the public bath with a bright red bag hanging from her mouth. This bag was filled with rice bran. When dipped in hot water, white liquid came from the bag and was used as soap. This is one of the ways in which kabuki incorporated daily customs of the Edo period to add a realistic touch. In turn, seeing how people dressed their hair and the cosmetics they used gives us a glimpse into a world totally different from today.

櫛　Combs

黒いたとう紙、つげ櫛、髪を結ぶ糸・元結は、髪を整えるときの道具です。
Tools for arranging hair: black *tattou* spread sheet, boxwood combs, *mottoi* (very strong cords to tie topknots).

合掌鏡台
Gassho ("Clasped Hands") Mirror and Stand

二枚の鏡が重なり合っていて、衿足などを合わせ鏡で見られるようになっています。
The mirrors come as a set of two, so that you can look in back and check the hair at the nape of neck.

手ぬぐい掛けと赤い糠袋
Tenugui handcloth on a stand and red *nuka-bukuro* bag

タオルのない時代、手を洗うところには手ぬぐい掛けが。
There was a stand with *tenugui* handcloths where you washed your hands.

『与話情浮名横櫛』お富（中村七之助）
Yowa Nasake Ukina no Yokogushi, Otomi (Nakamura Shichinosuke)

江戸時代の携帯化粧道具
Edo Period Portable Make-Up Tools

　こちらは実際に江戸時代の女性が懐に入れたり風呂敷に包んだりして持ち歩いた携帯用化粧道具。

　These are a make-up tools that were really used by Edo period women and could be tucked into one's kimono or carried in a cloth bundle.

板紅と紅筆
Rouge Palette and Rouge Brush

菊の蒔絵のお揃い。紅筆は押し出し式で蝶の取っ手がキュート。

All the items are decorated with a lacquered chrysanthemum pattern. The brush extends out by pushing a cute little button shaped like a butterfly.

手鏡
Hand Mirror

鏡は青銅の表面にメッキ処理をして反射面を作っていました。

The mirror is copper with a thin layer of shiny metal to make a reflective surface.

象牙の板紅　Ivory Rouge Palette

象牙に牡丹の透かし彫りがされたパレット式紅。懐や帯にさして持った携帯用です。

This rouge palette is ivory with a carved lattice of peony blossoms. It can be carried inside the kimono or slipped inside the obi.

携帯化粧道具
Portable Make-Up Kit

板紅、紅筆、白粉入れ、はけ、髪を整える櫛、毛抜き、手鏡の入った携帯化粧道具。

The set includes a rouge palette, rouge brush, container for white face make-up, *hake* puff, comb, tweezers to pluck hair and a hand mirror.

小町紅　"*Komachi* Rouge"

今も伊勢半本店によって、江戸時代の技が受け継がれ、紅花から作られる紅。玉虫色に輝く紅を水で溶いて使います。

This is still made by Isehan Honten using *beni* flowers with Edo period techniques. The solid make-up like a green *tamamushi* jewel beetle is thinned with water when it is used.

協力：(株)伊勢半本店 Courtesy of Isehan Honten　TEL：03-5774-0296　http://www.isehanhonten.co.jp

女形の鬘と髪飾り

Onnagata Wigs and Hair Ornaments

女形の髪形は衣裳とのバランスがとても大切。髪形と髪飾りも役柄、衣裳に合った色や大きさになっています。髪飾りの数や素材などで身分の違いやパターンを発見できます。それぞれ歌舞伎風に工夫はされていますが、江戸時代に実在した髪形です。幕末には、女性の日本髪のスタイルは二百数十種類もあったといいます。鬘の形、美しい髪飾りを見ているだけでも楽しいものです。

『新版歌祭文』に登場する裕福な商家の娘・お染と田舎の娘・お光は、主人公の久松をめぐる恋敵。身分の違いが髪形・髪飾りの素材や数に表れます。

A female character's hairstyle must balance her costume. The hair must fit the role type and the costume as well. The number of hair ornaments and the materials used indicate the social status of the character and there are all sorts of fascinating design motifs. Although slightly refined for kabuki, these hairstyles all actually existed in the Edo period. There were over two hundred different hairstyles for women at the end of the Edo period, most of them only remaining in kabuki.

In the play "*Shinpan Utazaimon*," popularly known as "Nozaki Village," Osome, the daughter of a wealthy merchant and Omitsu, a country girl, compete for the affections of Hisamatsu. The differences between these women from different classes can be seen in their costumes and their hair ornaments.

お光の鬘と髪飾り
The Wig and Ornaments for Omitsu

田舎の娘はシンプルで髪飾りの数が少ないのが特徴。
A country girl has just a few, simple hair ornaments.

朱の月型の櫛
Red moon-shaped comb

田舎娘の特徴、すすきの簪
A country girl has an ornamental hairpin suggesting pampas grass.

前髪を結ぶ赤の「すが糸」
"*Suga-ito* cords" tie up her front hair.

髷に巻きつける布「てがら」は鴇色の縮緬。
Omitsu's *tegara* cloth to decorate the topknot is *toki* light pink crepe silk.

お染の鬘と髪飾り

The Wig and Ornaments for Osome

裕福さを象徴する商家の娘の華やかな髪飾り。
The daughter of a wealthy merchant family has all sorts of colorful hair ornaments.

つまみ
Tsumami flower cluster hairpin

銀の丸ぴら
Silver hairpin with ornamental plate

色元結
Colored *mottoi* cords to tie the topknot

前髪の赤縮緬
Red *chirimen* crepe silk to tie the front hair

くす玉
Hairpin ornamented with a *kusudama* embroidered ball

鹿の子の「てがら」
Crepe silk *tegara* to decorate the topknot

箔置きの丈長
Paper *takenaga* ("long") ornaments with silver leaf for the topknot

人形じけ
Doll hanging side locks

つまみ簪、前ざし、ぴらぴら付き
Tiara comb decorated with flower clusters and silver bangles

基本的に、女形の鬘は重くて動きにくいもの。でも、美しくあるための我慢はできるものです。女性のおしゃれに対する意識は、今も昔も変わりません。

Wigs for *onnagata* are very heavy and it is difficult to move. But you have to endure it if you want to look beautiful. Women's feelings toward fashion are the same in the past and today.

染コメ‼ Somegoro's Comment

31

先笄
Sakkogai

江戸中期、上方の商家など裕福な女房たちの髪形。笄は女性が用いる棒状の髪飾り。

Around the 18th century, this was a hairstyle for wealthy merchant wives in Kamigata (the area around Kyoto and Osaka). A *kogai* is the ornamental rod used in women's hair.

髱 *Tabo* (lower back bun)

玉簪
Tama Kanzashi (Ornamental Hairpin Decorated with a Ball)

シンプルな玉簪。玉の大きさは役柄によって、また、鬘の大きさとのバランスで決まります。緑色は夏用。

These are simple ornamental hairpins. The size of the ball depends on the role type and also the balance with the size of the wig. This green ball is for summer.

傾城に
For a courtesan

芸者の夏用
For a geisha in summer

芸者に
For a geisha

年寄りの夏用
For an older woman in summer

庶民に
For a commoner

『お祭り』芸者（坂東玉三郎）
Omatsuri, Geisha (Bando Tamasaburo)

片はずし・しいたけ

Kata-hazushi (hair loose on one side), **Shiitake** (black mushroom)

御殿女中の中でも特に地位の高い武家の女たちの髪形。髻の部分が油で固められ「しいたけ」と呼ばれます。

This is the hairstyle for particularly high-ranking ladies-in-waiting in a samurai mansion. The *tabo* is hardened with wax and looks like a *shiitake* black mushroom.

『慇紅葉汗顔見勢』政岡（市川染五郎）
Haji Momiji Ase no Kaomise, Masaoka (Ichikawa Somegoro)

しいたけ
Shiitake (shaped like a *shiitake* black mushroom)

べっ甲の中ざし

Tortoiseshell Ornamental Rod

べっ甲の中ざしも役や髻の形、芝居の時代によって、大きさ、形などが違ってきます。

The size and shape of these tortoiseshell rods differ depending on the role, the shape of the bun and the age in which the play is set.

傾城に
For a courtesan

局、芸者に
For a *tsubone* high-ranking lady-in-waiting or a geisha

先笄、島田くずしに
For *sakkogai* or *Shimada kuzushi* hairstyles

元禄時代ものに
For plays set in the Genroku period at the beginning of the 18th century

「今様押絵鏡　芸者長吉」歌川豊国（三代）画・安政6（1859）年
"Geisha Chokichi" by Utagawa Toyokuni III (1859)

意味持つ女のかぶり物

Female Headgear with Special Meanings

女形のかぶり物はさまざまあります。手ぬぐいもその一つですが、その他にも女形ならではのかぶり物があります。それらは、それぞれに意味があり、お約束事の目印になっています。

There are all kinds of headgear for *onnagata*. *Tenugui* handcloths are one of them, but there are many others that are unique to *onnagata*. Each has a specific meaning and is a marker for what kind of stylization it is.

『仮名手本忠臣蔵』〈九段目〉本蔵妻戸無瀬（十八代目中村勘三郎）
Kanadehon Chushingura <Act IX>, Honzo's wife Tonase (Nakamura Kanzaburo XVIII)

角かくし

***Tsuno kakushi* ("Hiding the horns")**

現代では、「角かくし＝花嫁」ですが、実は角かくしは塵よけでした。つまり外出用の帽子のような役割だったようです。歌舞伎でも外出するときや旅をする「道行」の場面でよく見かけます。

Today this kind of cap is used for the bride's costume in a traditional wedding, but originally this is the kind of cap a woman wore to keep the dust off her hair when traveling. In kabuki this is often used when women are traveling or are on an outing.

紫帽子
purple *boshi* cap

画題不明
河原崎国太郎　歌川国貞（二代）
慶応元（1865）年
Print of onnagata Kawarasaki Kunitaro by
Utagawa Kunisada II (1865)

紫帽子
Purple *boshi* cap

鬘ができた頃、きれいに始末できない生え際を隠すためにつけたのが始まり。古典的な雰囲気を出すために紫帽子をつけます。紫帽子をつけるときは、丸い弧を描いた眉尻が帽子の中に隠れる「帽子眉」といわれる描き方をします。

When kabuki wigs were first developed, it was difficult to make the hairline look just right, so little patches of silk covered it. They are remnants of the caps that *onnagata* wore before wigs were used and give an atmosphere of kabuki's oldest age. When these patches of silk are used, there are special rounded eyebrows that are painted so the ends disappear under the cap.

紫鉢巻
Purple headband

左に結んで垂らしている紫色の鉢巻を「病鉢巻」といい、これは何かしら病気だというしるし。病気といっても恋わずらいのときも、本当に病気のときも、この病鉢巻をします。歌舞伎らしい、わかりやすい決まりごとです。

When the knot of this purple headband is tied on the character's left, it means the character is sick. Of course in kabuki, often this is illness that comes from love. But this headband was actually used to treat illnesses. Typically, kabuki made this into a convention visually stunning and instantly recognizable.

『廓文章』夕霧（坂田藤十郎）
Kuruwa Bunsho, Yugiri (Sakata Tojuro)

忠義のヒーロー　山伏スタイル

A Yamabushi Mountain Priest: A Loyal Hero

『勧進帳』弁慶（市川染五郎）　*Kanjincho*, Benkei (Ichikawa Somegoro)

歴代の名優が演じてきた『勧進帳』の弁慶は上演回数も多く、歌舞伎の定番でもあります。弁慶が扮する山伏とは修験道の僧のこと。市川格子（101ページ参照）という大胆な柄の着物、梵字の入った法衣、頭襟と呼ばれるかぶり物、金剛杖、扇などは、山伏の基本的なスタイルです。

Benkei in "*Kanjincho* (The Subscription List)" is a role that has been performed countless times by many famous actors. This is the fundamental style for a *yamabushi* mountain priest with a bold *Ichikawa* check (see page 101) patterned kimono, priest's robe with Sanscrit letters in gold-leaf, little *tokin* hat, *Kongo-zue* staff and fan.

美しき正義の浅葱色

Asagi Light-Blue, the Color of Virtue

『勧進帳』富樫（松本幸四郎）
Kanjincho, Togashi
(Matsumoto Koshiro)

情に厚くて頭がきれる『勧進帳』の富樫にぴったりの浅葱色の衣裳。弁慶に対峙したときの腰をどっしりと据えた爽やかな立ち姿を堪能いただきたいです。

浅葱色は死を覚悟した場面に使われることが多く（44ページ参照）、武士の情けで源義経の一行の通行を許した瞬間に、富樫が死を覚悟したであろう心情をも表しています。

Togashi, the barrier keeper in "*Kanjincho*" is virtuous and loyal and the light-blue (*asagi*) of his kimono fits his character perfectly. He confronts Benkei without wavering.

In kabuki, *asagi* is often used for characters who have decided on death (see page 44). This suggests that when Togashi lets Yoshitsune and his party through the barrier with the mercy of a warrior, he is prepared to take responsibility for this with death.

松革菱に鶴と亀の模様を散らした素襖に長袴。惚れ惚れするような、とても舞台映えのする色です。
Togashi wears a large sleeved *suo* robe and long *naga bakama* trousers with a pattern of diamonds of pine bark together with cranes and tortoises.

歌舞伎ヒーローの戦闘服

Fighting Gear for a Kabuki Hero

『暫』鎌倉権五郎（市川海老蔵）　Shibaraku, Kamakura Gongoro (Ichikawa Ebizo)

『暫』の鎌倉権五郎は、弱い民衆を苦しめる悪人に立ち向かうスーパーヒーロー。見せ場は、このいでたちで花道から出てくる場面。怒りを表現した隈取の「筋隈」（88ページ参照）、鬘、衣裳、小道具すべてにおいて大きく、強さを強調したスーパーぶりに驚きます。長い大太刀でバッタバッタと悪人を倒す、単純明快、文句なしに観て楽しめる代表的な荒事＊です。

Kamakura Gongoro in "*Shibaraku* (Wait a Moment!)" is a super hero who fights for the weak against powerful evil men. When he appears on the *hanamichi*, everything, including *suji-guma* (*kumadori* in lines, see page 88) make-up expressing righteous anger, exaggerated wig, costume and props show his scale. He cuts down all the villains with an enormous sword. This is the bombastic *aragoto*＊ style that is enjoyable and easy to understand.

＊荒事：荒々しく豪快な演技や演目をいう。
　Aragoto : *Aragoto* are plays and the acting style featuring larger-than-life heroes with exaggerated staging.

『助六由縁江戸桜』助六（十二代目市川團十郎）
Sukeroku Yukari no Edo Zakura,
Sukeroku (Ichikawa Danjuro XII)

花道に花が咲いたように美しい蛇の目傘
A *janome* umbrella like a blossoming flower

背中には尺八
Tucked in back,
a *shakuhachi* flute

牡丹の印籠
Inro case
with peony design

男伊達下駄
Otoko date geta clogs

刀
Sword

　豪快で強くて華のある『助六由縁江戸桜』の助六は歌舞伎一男前。美しい蛇の目傘を持って出てきて、花道で見せる見得には心奪われます。お芝居そのものも、江戸荒事の完成形として舞台が美しいのはもちろんですが、衣裳の黒、赤、紫のコントラストに、完成された歌舞伎美を感じます。

　This is Sukeroku, powerful and colorful, the kabuki model of a sleek leading man. His handsome *mie* poses on the *hanamichi* with a beautiful purple *janome* umbrella will take your breath away. The story and staging show Edo *aragoto* kabuki in its perfected form and the contrast of colors in Sukeroku's costume:black, red and purple exemplify the aesthetic of kabuki.

綸子の光沢　殿様の品格

A Lord's Dignity in the Sheen of Figured Silk

高貴な殿様は、たいてい紗綾形の地模様のある上品な綸子の着物です。お揃いの羽織を着ると貫禄と大きさを感じさせます。光沢のある綸子は、庶民には手の届かないもの。幾重にも重ねた衿元、たっぷり真綿が入った裾を上手にさばきながら座る姿にも殿様らしさが出ています。

High ranking samurai lords usually wear kimonos of *rinzu* silk figured with a diamond *sayagata* pattern. This shiny *rinzu* silk would have been out of reach for most commoners. The grace of a samurai lord shows through the movements with this kimono with many layers showing at the lapels and with thick padding at the bottom hem.

『元禄忠臣蔵』〈御浜御殿綱豊卿〉綱豊卿（片岡仁左衛門）
Genroku Chushingura <Ohama Goten Tsunatoyo Kyo>, Lord Tsunatoyo (Kataoka Nizaemon)

『元禄忠臣蔵』〈御浜御殿綱豊卿〉の綱豊卿。草色の着物の美しさに惚れ惚れします。演じる役者には品格と存在感が必要になります。
This is Lord Tsunatoyo in the "*Ohama Goten Tsunatoyo Kyo*" scene of "*Genroku Chushingura*." The beauty of this green colored kimono is entrancing and the actor must have dignity and presence to match it.

綸子の着流しは、いわゆる殿様の普段着です。本当に上品で素敵な着物なので、楽屋で身に着けただけで、とても気持ちがよいのです。

This is casual wear for a samurai lord. This is really an elegant costume and it feels wonderful even just putting it on in the dressing room.

 染コメ!! Somegoro's Comment

立役の中でもっとも華やかなのが若衆の衣裳です。武士の中でも前髪があるのが、成人していない男子、若衆です。その衣裳は色も緋色や鴇色、刺しゅうでお花いっぱいといった、女形顔負けのかわいらしさです。芝居の中で、時には男に、時には女に惚れられるイケメンたちです。

The most colorful *tachiyaku* male roles are those for *wakashu* youths. Instead of having the shaved top of the head of an adult samurai, samurai youths retain their forelock of hair. Their costumes are *hiiro* scarlet or *toki* light pink and have colorful embroidered patterns. *Wakashu* are colorful and attractive and can make both men and women fall in love with them.

『本朝廿四孝』〈十種香〉武田勝頼の紫の長袴に緋色の着物。業平菱という文様に鳳凰。役者さんによって鴇色の着物を着ることもあります。
This is the costume Takeda Katsuyori wears in "*Honcho Nijushiko*," with purple *naga bakama* trousers and a scarlet kimono. The embroidered pattern is a diamond shaped mesh called "*Narihira-bishi*" with phoenixes. With some actors, the kimono is a light pink.

敬意を込めて役者の家紋

Family Crests of a Revered Actor of the Past

歌舞伎の衣裳には、そのとき演じる役者さんの紋を入れているものがありますが、誰が演じても同じ紋をつける場合があります。これはかつて、その役を当たり役として完成させた役者の紋で、先人たちの偉大さをたたえ、敬意を表しているのです。

There are some costumes that always have the same family crests, no matter who is playing the role. These are the family crests of the actor who perfected that role and his crests are used out of reverence for that actor.

「伊達競高評鞘当 仁木弾正 坂東彦三郎」
歌川豊国(三代)画 安政五(1858)年
Bando Hikosaburo as Nikki Danjo by Utagawa Toyokuni III (1858).

『伽羅先代萩』〈床下〉の仁木弾正は、五代目松本幸四郎の当たり役とされ、誰が演じても裃には高麗屋の三ツ銀杏の五つ紋、裃袴は四ツ花菱の柄になっていて、同じ衣裳です。
The role of the villain Nikki Danjo in "*Meiboku Sendai Hagi*" was perfected by Matsumoto Koshiro V (1764 – 1838) and has his *mitsu-icho* (three gingko leaves) crests and a pattern of his *yotsu-hanabishi* (four flower diamonds) crest.

僕にとって仁木弾正は特別です。五代目幸四郎に敬意を表して、現在まであらゆる役者さんが着てきた衣裳。高麗屋の僕がこの衣裳を着るというだけで、鳥肌が立つほどゾクゾクします。

Whoever plays the role of Nikki Danjo, the actor always uses this costume covered with the crests of Koshiro V. Since he is a great ancestor in my acting family, just putting on the costume gives me goose bumps.

 染コメ!! Somegoro's Comment

これぞ武士のフォーマル

烏帽子をかぶり、袖と背中に大きな紋のついた素襖、長袴。これが江戸時代の大名の第一礼装でした。武士の礼装は、主君の権力維持のため、また忠誠心の証でもあったわけです。

In the Edo period, the most formal robes for a samurai lord were large *suo* robes with the lord's crest on the sleeves and back, extremely long *naga-bakama* trousers and tall *eboshi* court cap. These robes both symbolized the power of the lord and his loyalty to the shogun.

塩冶判官の衣裳、2m25cmもある長袴は、殿中での不穏な動きや争い事を防ぐためとか。役者は大きく見せると同時に裾さばきをよくするために高さのある履物を履くことも。

The costume for Enya Hangan features *naga-bakama* 2 m. 25 cm. long. One explanation for this clothing is that it prevented violence inside the shogun's palace. To make the actor look large and to make it easier to walk, the actor wears footwear inside.

『仮名手本忠臣蔵』〈大序〉では、色とりどりの第一礼装が並びます。大紋に長袴を身に着け、悠然と動く姿がきれいです。
In the great prologue to "*Kanadehon Chushingura*," the three main characters wear these robes and their colors show their differing personalities.

『仮名手本忠臣蔵』〈大序〉桃井若狭之助(市川染五郎)、塩冶判官(尾上菊之助)、高師直(市川海老蔵)
Kanadehon Chushingura<Great Prologue>, Momonoi Wakasanosuke (Ichikawa Somegoro), Enya Hangan (Onoe Kikunosuke), Ko no Morono (Ichikawa Ebizo)

長袴で歩くときは、すり足で歩くことが基本です。靴で歩くように足をあげると、うまく歩けません。袴の長さを意識しながら、ゆったりと優雅に歩くようにします。

When walking in *naga-bakama*, you have to use the *suri-ashi* sliding step. If you try to walk like you are wearing shoes, it won't work. You walk slowly and elegantly, always keeping the length of the *hakama* in mind.

染コメ!! Somegoro's Comment

武士の誇り　浅葱の紋服

Samurai Pride: *Asagi* Kimono with Family Crests

『仮名手本忠臣蔵』〈六段目〉の勘平は家に帰るとこの浅葱色の紋服に着替え、刀の大小をさし切腹します。色男にはこの色が似合います。「武士として死ぬ」というプライドをかけた気持ちを演出した衣裳でもあるのです。

In the sixth act of "*Chushingura* (The Treasury of Loyal Retainers)," Kanpei, a samurai in disgrace, comes home and immediately changes from hunting clothes into his formal samurai kimono, and puts on his two swords. The light-blue *asagi* color is flattering to a good looking man, but, as in many other cases in kabuki, also suggests Kanpei's determination to die as a samurai.

『仮名手本忠臣蔵』〈六段目〉早野勘平 (尾上菊五郎)
Kanadehon Chushingura <Act VI>, Hayano Kanpei (Onoe Kikugoro).

シンプルな無地の衣裳ですが、この勘平の浅葱色に染めるのが難しく、衣裳さんは色出しに苦労するそうです。
This kimono is only dyed silk without patterns, but it is difficult to get the cloth the proper color.

切腹は、武士だけに許される「名誉ある死」です。その特別な儀式の際は、身を清め、それにふさわしい着物を身に着けます。『元禄忠臣蔵』(げんろくちゅうしんぐら)の大石内蔵助(のすけ)が身に着けている死装束(しにしょうぞく)は、白無地の小袖(こそで)に浅葱色(あさぎ)の麻の裃。この美しい姿、表情から、大石の静かで力強い覚悟が伝わってきます。

Seppuku ritual suicide was considered an honorable death restricted to samurai. There were many rituals and proper clothing for it. The clothing that Oishi Kuranosuke wears in *"Genroku Chushingura"* for his ritual suicide has a white unpatterned kimono with very light *asagi* colored linen *kamishimo* shoulder pieces and *hakama* divided skirt. This beautiful costume and his calm expression shows Oishi Kuranosuke's strong resolution as he goes to his death.

『元禄忠臣蔵』2006年12月公演国立劇場ポスター
提供・国立劇場／大石内蔵助・松本幸四郎／撮影・加藤孝／デザイン・阿部壽／題字・閑万希子
Poster for *"Genroku Chushingura"* at the National Theatre of Japan in December 2006.
Courtesy of the National Theatre of Japan./Matsumoto Koshiro as Oishi Kuranosuke/Photograph by Kato Takashi/Poster design by Abe Hisashi/Calligraphy by Kan Makiko

色気漂う悪の黒

Black: Evil and Sexy

歌舞伎の黒には、黒衣*のように「無」を表している黒と「悪の香り」漂う黒とがあります。一般に黒は地味で暗い色ですが、歌舞伎の衣裳で使われる黒は自己主張のある強い色です。白塗りに黒の着物の絶妙なコントラストが生み出す美しさと色気。退廃的な浪人風だと女心がさらにゆさぶられます。

There are two blacks, the black that means "nothingness" as with *kurogo** and the black that gives off the aroma of evil. In kabuki, black is a strong color that accentuates an actor's presence. This is the sex appeal created by the contrast between pure white make-up and a black kimono. If the character is a decadent *ronin* master-less samurai, he is even sexier.

『東海道四谷怪談』民谷伊右衛門（市川染五郎）
Tokaido Yotsuya Kaidan, Tamiya Iemon (Ichikawa Somegoro)

歌舞伎の極彩色の中で、黒は特別。陰のある色気が漂います。黒の衣裳はほとんど紋付で、落ちぶれてもお家や武士のプライドを感じさせます。

Black has a dark eroticism different from all the other colors in kabuki. A formal black kimono with family crests emphasizes the feeling that even down and out, a samurai has his pride and clings to the prestige of his clan.

染コメ!! Somegoro's Comment

『東海道四谷怪談』民谷伊右衛門は、金のためなら人殺しだって、妻子を捨てることだってできる……極悪非道の男、でも男前。〈隠亡堀〉の場面での黒紋付の着流しが色っぽい。

In "*Yotsuya Kaidan* (The Ghosts of Yotsuya)" Tamiya Iemon is cruel and heartless and will do anything for money: kill people, abandon his wife and child. In the "*Onbobori*" scene, his black crested kimono looks very sexy.

『義経千本桜』〈渡海屋〉の知盛は純白とシルバーの狩衣で登場し、〈大物浦〉で、狩衣を血に染めながら襲いかかる姿は、生きているか死んでいるかわからないような妖しさ。このシルバーと血の色のコントラストが視覚に強烈で、知盛の執念や絶望や無念が伝わってきます。

In the "*Tokaiya*" and "*Daimotsu* Bay" scenes of "Yoshitsune and the Thousand Cherry Trees," Tomomori appears in a magnificent pure white and silver *kariginu* court robe which then is stained bright red with blood. Strangely, Tomomori looks both dead and alive. The impact of the contrast of the white and silver and blood red conveys Tomomori's thirst for vengeance, despair and frustration.

『義経千本桜』〈渡海屋・大物浦〉知盛（松本幸四郎）
Yoshitsune Senbonzakura <Tokaiya, Daimotsu no Ura>, Tomomori (Matsumoto Koshiro)

47

はんなりお決まり若旦那

わかだんな

Waka Danna Young Master: Elegant, Cheerful and Undependable

お調子者だけど憎めない、性格悪いけど色男……。そんな女心をくすぐるのが商家の若旦那たち。どのお芝居でも、たいてい同じような着物と羽織を着ています。この若旦那が美しい女に

見惚れて羽織を落としてしまう「羽織落とし」と呼ばれる場面があります。羽織の裏地には演じる役者さんの紋にちなんだ柄がちゃんと染められているのでお見逃しなく。

A *waka danna*, the young master of a wealthy merchant family is convivial, but likable, thoroughly undependable, but attractive and good looking and irresistible to women. He usually wears matching kimono and *haori* coat and there is a routine where he unconsciously strips off this coat when he sees a beautiful woman and falls in love with her. The costume is specially made for the actor and the pattern, especially the lining of the *haori* is usually a fashionable version of the actor's crest.

『与話情浮名横櫛』〈木更津海岸見染〉与三郎（市川染五郎）
Yowa Nasake Ukina no Yokogushi <Kisarazu Kaigan Misome>, Yosaburo (Ichikawa Somegoro)

世間知らずの若旦那といえば『与話情浮名横櫛』の与三郎。はんなり優しい縮緬の着物。羽織の裏地は高麗屋の家紋・三ツ銀杏の吹き寄せ柄。
The kimono for Yosaburo in the first part of "Scarfaced Yosaburo" is crepe silk. The lining of the *haori* coat has a pattern of the Koraiya crest of three gingko leaves.

『恋飛脚大和往来』〈新口村〉梅川（片岡孝太郎）／忠兵衛（市川染五郎）
Koibikyaku Yamato Orai <Ninokuchi-mura>, Umegawa (Kataoka Takataro) / Chubei (Ichikawa Somegoro)

『恋飛脚大和往来』〈新口村〉の忠兵衛と梅川。真っ白な雪の舞台に、黒地に流水と梅の裾模様。紋は役者2人の紋を並べた比翼紋になっています。

In "*Ninokuchi-mura*," the formal black kimonos of Chubei and Umegawa contrast with the snow. The bottom halves have designs of plum blossoms and streams. The linked crests are the crests of the actors playing the roles.

　歌舞伎で男女がペアルックを着るのは、身分違いの恋やら、罪を犯した逃避行やら、何かしらの理由で心中しようとするときです。このとき、衣裳にはお揃いの柄と比翼の紋が。死を覚悟し思いつめた2人の姿が、とてもはかなく胸がしめつけられます。

　When a pair of lovers wear matching kimonos, they are usually going to love suicide because they come from different classes or have committed some crime. They wear matching kimonos with linked crests called "hiyoku no mon." The matching kimonos make the lovers look all the more poignant.

引き立て合う揃(ぞろ)いの衣裳

Matching Kimonos that Amplify Each Other

《白浪五人男(しらなみ ごにんおとこ)》で知られる『青砥稿花紅彩画(あおとぞうしはなのにしきえ)』〈稲瀬川(いなせがわ)〉の場では5人の盗賊が花道にずらっと並び、盗賊になった生い立ちを語ります。小気味のいい七五調の台詞、それぞれ役柄にちなんだ着物の柄つけに注目です。

In the "Inase River" scene of "*Shiranami Gonin Otoko* (The Five Thieves)," the five thieves line up and recount their backgrounds all in beautiful poetic language. They wear magnificent matching kimonos with design motifs suited to their characters.

役者から見ても白浪五人男はかっこいいと思います。同じ着物に帯は貝の口ですが、その役の個性に合わせて、衣裳さんが着付け方、帯の結び方を微妙に変えています。そんなところもじっくり見てほしいと思います。

Even for the actors, "*Shiranami Gonin Otoko*" is very interesting. For example, the obis are all tied with the same *kai no kuchi* knot. But the costumers vary the knots very slightly to give the feeling of the different characters. Keep an eye out for this detail.

 染コメ‼ Somegoro's Comment

『青砥稿花紅彩画』左から、日本駄右衛門（市川左團次）、南郷力丸（中村獅童）、赤星十三郎（市川春猿）、忠信利平（市川段治郎）、弁天小僧菊之助（市川海老蔵）

Aoto Zoshi Hana no Nishiki-e, from left, Nippon Daemon (Ichikawa Sadanji), Nango Rikimaru (Nakamura Shido), Akaboshi Juzaburo (Ichikawa Shun'en), Tadanobu Rihei (Ichikawa Danjiro), Benten Kozo Kikunosuke (Ichikawa Ebizo)

帯結び（貝の口）
Kai no kuchi type of *obi* knot

日本駄右衛門の衣裳は、白浪の裾模様と肩に描かれた方位磁石。南郷力丸の衣裳は、稲妻の模様と雷獣の図。赤星十三郎の衣裳は、尾長鶏に星の図。忠信利平の衣裳は、大胆な雲模様に龍。弁天小僧菊之助の衣裳は、菊に白蛇。

Nippon Daemon's costume has a pattern of white waves on the bottom and a compass attached to a rope on his shoulders.
Nango Rikimaru's costume has storm clouds and a thunder beast.
Akaboshi Juzaburo's costume has a long-tailed cock and a star.
Tadanobu Rihei's costume has a bold pattern of clouds and a dragon.
Benten Kozo's costume has a pattern of chrysanthemums and a white snake.

歌舞伎の衣裳には、ストレートに役名そのままの柄になっている衣裳があります。『菅原伝授手習鑑』〈車引〉に登場する三兄弟には、それぞれ木の名前がついています。松王丸、梅王丸、桜丸が着物の肩肌を脱ぐと、それぞれの名前のモチーフの文様。そして、〈賀の祝〉の場面では、それぞれの女房たちも夫の名にちなんだモチーフの文様の着物を着ています。

There are kabuki costumes that directly incorporate images in the character's name into the costume. In the *"Kurumabiki* (The Fight Over the Carriage)" scene of *"Sugawara Denju Tenarai Kagami* (Sugawara and Secrets of Calligraphy)," there are triplets all named after trees: the pine, the plum and the cherry. Their under-kimonos all have these motifs on them. Then, in the following *"Ga no Iwai* (The Birthday Celebration)" scene, their wives also have motifs relating to their husbands' names.

桜丸
Sakuramaru ("*sakura*" = "cherry")

梅王丸
Umeomaru ("*ume*" = "plum")

桜、梅、松のモチーフに一つひとつ綿を入れて縫い付け、立体的な華やかさを出しています。
To emphasize them, the floral motifs are on separate pieces of cloth that are sewn on with lots of cotton batting behind.

3人の女房たちの衣裳
Costumes of the three wives

『菅原伝授手習鑑』〈賀の祝〉に登場する3人の女房の着物。
The names and kimonos of the three wives are related to their husbands' names.

八重　Yae
桜丸の妻・八重は藤色に春らしい春草柄。
The wife of Sakuramaru (= "cherry") is Yae (a kind of cherry) and her kimono is lavender with spring motifs.

春　Haru
梅王丸の妻・春は、薄納戸色に梅の花の裾模様。
The wife of Umeomaru (= "plum") is Haru (= "spring") and her kimono is light blue with a pattern of plum blossoms.

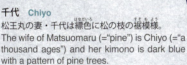

千代　Chiyo
松王丸の妻・千代は縹色に松の枝の裾模様。
The wife of Matsuomaru (="pine") is Chiyo (="a thousand ages") and her kimono is dark blue with a pattern of pine trees.

松王丸
Matsuomaru ("*matsu*" = "pine")

〈車引〉のおなじみの衣裳ですが、役者さんによっては、三兄弟とも緋色の衣裳で、桜丸の化粧には隈取がないこともあります。それだけでもずいぶん印象が違うものです。

"*Kurumabiki* (The Fight Over the Carriage)" appears all the time, but details can change according to the actor. For example, all three brothers might have red kimonos, or Sakuramaru's make-up may not have *kumadori*. Just these little changes can change the impression entirely.

染コメ‼ Somegoro's Comment

誰もが大きくなれる肉襦袢

Niku-Juban Flesh Costume: Anyone Can Become a Muscleman

普通の体格の役者が力士や大男を演じるために身に着ける肉襦袢。着物の中に分厚い綿の入った補正着を着たり、着ぐるみのようなものを着たりして身体を大きく見せています。実際の舞台の上でぐっと大きく見えるのは、もちろん肉襦袢効果もありますが、動き方や座り方にも、大きく見える工夫がされているのです。

When an actor of ordinary build has to play a sumo wrestler or large man, he pads his body with a suit called a *niku-juban*. This is a body suit with cotton padding to make a person look large. Of course, when on stage, this is amplified by the way of moving and sitting.

「濡髪長五郎」歌川豊国（三代）画
"Nuregami Chogoro" by Utagawa Toyokuni Ⅲ.

『双蝶々曲輪日記』〈角力場〉濡髪長五郎（市川染五郎）
Futatsu Chocho Kuruwa Nikki <Sumoba>, Nuregami Chogoro (Ichikawa Somegoro)

『双蝶々曲輪日記』〈角力場〉の濡髪長五郎は当代一の相撲取り。その立派さを表すために、戸口から出てくるとき、足元に台を置いて大きく見せたり、座るときも合引＊に座って大きく見えるようにしたりして工夫しています。

Nuregami Chogoro in *"Futatsu Chocho Kuruwa Nikki"* is the role of a top sumo wrestler. To look big, going through a door, he stands on a box so he must bend way over. Then, when sitting, there is an extra *aibiki* box under him to make him look big.

 染コメ!! Somegoro's Comment

＊合引：役者を大きく見せるために用いる腰掛や箱。93ページ参照。
Aibiki: seats or boxes that make the actor look good. see page 93.

『夏祭浪花鑑』団七九郎兵衛（片岡愛之助）
Natsu Matsuri Naniwa Kagami, Danshichi Kurobei (Kataoka Ainosuke)

元々、赤いふんどしは護身用。海で鮫に出会ったとき、赤いふんどしをほどいて泳ぐと、鮫は自分より長いものは飲み込めないと思い襲わないのだそうです。
Originally, red loincloths were for protection. When you encountered a shark while in the sea, you would swim away while untying your loincloth. The shark would realize it couldn't swallow something longer than itself and wouldn't attack.

歌舞伎では、着物の裾をからげて「尻っぱしょり」をし、ふんどしをちらりと見せる、なんとも男の色気を感じさせる場面がたくさんあります。ふんどしの色にも意味があり、赤はとても粋で鰯背、黒や鼠色は汚れていることを表現しているのだそうです。

Often a male character tucks up the hem of the kimono, a style called "*shirippashori*", and the front flap of the loincloth peeks out, with a masculine allure. The color of the loincloth has meaning. Red is for a gallant, powerful man, black or grey suggests a dirty loincloth.

江戸の男のちらリズム
The Pride of an Edo Man Peeks Out

鬘でわかる立役の身分

Wigs for *Tachiyaku* Roles of Different Status

立役の鬘は髪飾りがあるわけでないので一見、地味ですが、役の数だけ種類があり、実は鬘の形が役の身分や性根まで物語っています。

Wigs for *tachiyaku* male roles all look the same at first, after all, there are few accessories, but there are many types of wigs for characters from different social stations and with different personalities.

『与話情浮名横櫛』〈木更津海岸見初染〉与三郎（市川染五郎）
Yowa Nasake Ukina no Yokogushi <Kisarazu Kaigan Misome>,
Yosaburo (Ichikawa Somegoro)

二枚目 *Nimaime* (Handsome Young Man)

二枚目のトレードマークは、二つ折という古風な色男の髷の形です。
The trademark of the *nimaime* is the bend in the topknot called "*futatsu-ori.*"

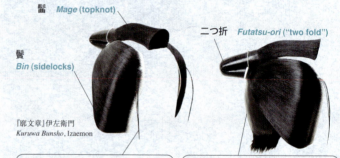

髷 *Mage* (topknot)

鬢 *Bin* (sidelocks)

二つ折 *Futatsu-ori* ("two fold")

『廓文章』伊左衛門
Kuruwa Bunsho, Izaemon

しけ *Shike* ("loose hair")
鬢からたれる一筋の髪をしけといい、この一筋の髪だけで色気が漂います。
Stray strands of hair from an otherwise perfectly groomed wig are called "*shike*" and add allure.

油付 *Abura-tsuki* ("oil attached")
鬢の後ろの部分（髱）を油で固めた状態を油付と呼びます。
When the back hair of the wig ("*tabo*") is hardened with wax it is described as "*abura-tsuki.*"

お殿様

Otono-sama (Samurai Lord)

大名という名前の、大名の典型的な鬘の形です。
This is the classical wig for a *daimyo* samurai lord and is even called, "*daimyo.*"

この角度を控えます。
The topknot is at this angle.

『伽羅先代萩』細川勝元 *Meiboku Sendaihagi*, Hosokawa Katsumoto

『梶原平三誉石切』梶原平三の髷も生締。
The wig for Kajiwara in "Ishikiri Kajiwara (Stonecutting Kajiwara)" is a *nama-jime*.

『梶原平三誉石切』梶原平三（中村吉右衛門）
Kajiwara Heizo Homare no Ishikiri, Kajiwara Heizo (Nakamura Kichiemon)

捌き役
Sabaki yaku (Men of Judgment)

生締　*Nama-jime* ("raw tie")
生締は捌き役などによく用いられる髷の形。
This thick topknot hardened with wax is called "*nama-jime*" and is often used for mature men of judgment.

《金閣寺》此下東吉
Kinkakuji, Konoshita Tokichi

ちりちり　*Chiri-chiri*
髷の根元や鬢の上の部分についているのは、針金を巻いて、漆で焼いたもの。強さを表現しています。
These curls indicate strength and are created by hardening coils of wire with lacquer and are applied to the base of the topknot or on the sidelocks.

『元禄忠臣蔵』〈御浜御殿綱豊卿〉
綱豊卿（片岡仁左衛門）
Genroku Chushingura <Ohama Goten Tsunatoyo Kyo>, Lord Tsunatoyo (Kataoka Nizaemon)

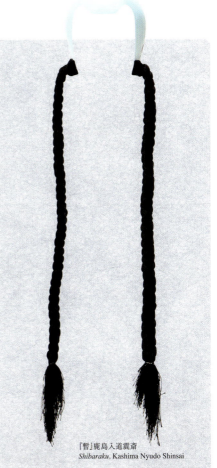

『暫』鹿島入道震斎
Shibaraku, Kashima Nyudo Shinsai

なまず坊主
Namazu Bozu ("catfish priest")
言葉そのまま丸坊主のこと。三つ編みになっているのは絹糸で作られたもみあげです。
The wig itself is for a Buddhist priest with shaved head, but this particular one has long whiskers, which are made of braids of silk cords.

『伽羅先代萩』〈床下〉荒獅子男之助
Meiboku Sendai Hagi <Yukashita>, Arajishi Otokonosuke

荒事*・強い役
Aragoto* and Other Powerful Roles

鬢はヤクの毛を使って漆で固めていて、アクの強い役、力強い役に用います。

The *bin* sidelocks are made of yak hair hardened with lacquer. This is used for powerful roles and roles with strong personalities.

『八犬傳 犬の草帋の内 犬飼現八信道』
歌川国貞（二代）画／嘉永5(1852)年
"Inukai Genpachi from *Hakkenden*" by Utagawa Kunisada II(1852).

位の高い武士
High-Ranking Samurai

棒茶筅　*Bo Chasen* ("Pole Tea Whisk")

大将など位の高い武士の髷で、茶道で使う茶筅のイメージから名づけられました。打紐でぐるぐる巻いて立派です。

This topknot looks like the bamboo whisk used in the tea ceremony. It looks very grand wrapped with cord.

「八犬傳 犬之草帋之内 足利成氏」歌川国貞（二代）画／嘉永5(1852)年
"Ashikaga Nariuji from *Hakkenden*" by Utagawa Kunisada II(1852).

『伽羅先代萩』〈花水橋〉足利頼兼
Meiboku Sendai Hagi <Hanamizu Bashi>, Ashikaga Yorikane

相撲取り

Sumo Wrestler

相撲取りの鬘のひとつの小野川銀杏。特にこれは「がったり風」の鬘。誰かと争った後や走ってきたという場面で、髪が乱れて髷が曲がったり、下がったりしていることを表現しています。

One wig for a sumo wrestler is called "Onogawa Gingko." This particular form is called "gattari-fu" and is used after the character has been fighting or running and his hair is disordered.

『双蝶々曲輪日記』〈角力場〉濡髪長五郎（市川染五郎）
Futatsu Chocho Kuruwa Nikki <Sumoba>, Nuregami Chogoro (Ichikawa Somegoro)

『伽羅先代萩』〈花水橋〉相撲取り・絹川谷蔵
Meiboku Sendai Hagi, <Hanamizu Bashi> sumo wrestler Kinugawa

髷次第で、顔の輪郭が違って見えます。くり（額の生え際）が1mm、2mm違うだけで印象が全然違うのです。髪はその家それぞれ、役者それぞれが鬘屋さん、床山さんと一緒に研究して、自分に合った形を見つけていきます。

A wig can totally change the outline of an actor's face. Just 1 or 2 mm at the kuri (hairline), can make all the difference in the world. Actors work with the katsura-ya (wig maker) and tokoyama (wig dresser) to find the perfect wig for them.

 染コメ‼ Somegoro's Comment

むしり　Mushiri (grown out hair)

月代が伸びている状態のことをむしりといいます。

When the shaved top of the head grows out, the bushy look is called "mushiri."

『於染久松色読販』鬼門の喜兵衛
Osome Hisamatsu Ukina no Yomiuri, Kimon no Kihei

御家人・敵役

Out of Luck Samurai and Villains

鬘を油などで固めず、きちんと手入れもされず何十日も月代が伸びている状態から、落ちぶれた御家人、敵役に用います。

For samurai who are in poor circumstances and can't groom their back hair with wax or shave the tops of their heads, these wigs are used. Often these are villainous roles.

袋付　Fukuro-tsuki (unhardened back hair)

鬘を油などで固めていない状態のこと。

Fukuro-tsuki ("bag" back hair) is when the back hair is made into a bun, and is not hardened with wax.

役に応じた　カラフル足袋

Colorful *Tabi* for All Kinds of Different Roles

一般的に、足袋は自分の足のサイズにぴったり合った、しわひとつないのが美しいとされています。足袋は自分のサイズにぴったりこないと気持ちが悪いもの。毎月、衣裳さんが役者さんにぴったり合うサイズで、役に応じた足袋をその都度用意されるのだそうです。そして、時には1か月の公演中に、何足も履きつぶしてしまうこともあるそうです。

　歌舞伎には、いろいろな色の足袋が登場します。茶坊主や敵役の赤っ面は黄色、奴衆は紫色、職人は藍色と、歌舞伎の中でもゆるい傾向があるように思います

Tabi are socks with a slit between the big toe and the rest of the toes. To feel right, *tabi* need to fit your feet exactly, so star actors use *tabi* tailored to their feet. It looks most beautiful when they fit tightly without a single wrinkle. In a single month of performances, an actor wears out many pairs of *tabi*.

Kabuki uses *tabi* in all kinds of colors. In kabuki there are some vague guidelines for colors for roles. There are yellow *tabi* for tea priests and villains with red faces, purple *tabi* for samurai footmen and dark blue *tabi* for craftsmen. But since the 14th century, samurai society had very strict rules for

が、室町時代以降、武家では足袋の規制
が厳しく、なんと許可制だったのです。
御殿女中でも病人でも足袋を履くには許
可が必要となり、足袋を履く時期も決め
られていたそうです。主君の前では素足
が正式だったとは意外です。江戸時代は
ある程度、職業によっても足袋の色が決
まっていたともいわれます。町人が履く
足袋はかなり自由だったようで、色にも
流行があったそうです。

　また、遊女や花魁は足袋を履いていま
せん。素足の美しさは遊女の売りで、足
袋は野暮だと履かなかったようです。

the use of *tabi*. Even women serving
in the shogun's palace and sick people
could not wear *tabi* without special
permission. In fact, surprisingly, it was
considered a sign of loyalty to appear
barefoot in the presence of your lord.
In general, the restrictions on *tabi*
didn't apply to commoners, so there
were all kinds of fashion trends in colors of *tabi*.

　Also, in kabuki and real life, prostitutes and courtesans do not wear *tabi*.
That is because beautiful feet were
part of the attraction of courtesans and
it was considered bad to cover them
with *tabi*.

食べ物
Food

歌舞伎では、いろいろな食べ物が登場します。とてもリアルに工夫して作られています。中には一部、本物の食べ物もあって、実際に食べるシーンも。

今ではあまり見かけない、その時代を思わせる食べ物、また忘れかけていた季節感や情緒を思い出させてくれるものもあります。

All kinds of foods appear in kabuki plays. There are props that are made to look very real, but sometimes there are things that are really eaten on stage. There are all kinds of things that show us what life was like in the Edo period in commoner neighborhoods and remind us of seasonal delicacies.

お膳
Ozen (A Dinner Table with Food)

『仮名手本忠臣蔵』〈七段目・祇園一力茶屋〉に登場するお膳。役者がお膳のおさしみをおいしそうに食べるシーンがあります。このおさしみ、実は羊羹。甘いおさしみです。

In the "*Ichiriki* Teahouse" scene of "*Chushingura*," this table of food appears. When actors eat *sashimi* raw fish, they are actually eating slices of *yokan* sweet been jelly. Very sweet *sashimi*!

そば
Soba (buckwheat noodles)

『雪暮夜入谷畦道』《直侍》の〈入谷そば屋〉の場、
直次郎が熱々のおそばで冷えた体を温めます。そ
ばを食べる場面があるとき、どんぶりは小道具さ
んが用意し、おそばは その劇場の中または周辺の
そば屋から毎日、出前で届けられます。1階の1
列目に座ると、ほのかにだしの香りがしてくるこ
ともあります。

In the "*Soba* Shop" scene of "*Yuki no Yube
Iriya no Azemichi*," the thief Naojiro is on the
run and stops to warm himself up with some
soba noodles. When an actor has to actually
eat noodles on stage, the prop man prepares
the bowl, but the noodles are delivered by a
shop in the theater or nearby, and from the
front seats, you can even smell the broth.

初鰹
Hatsu-Gatsuo (The First Bonito Fish of the Season)

『梅雨小袖昔八丈』《髪結新三》で湯屋帰りの新三が高値
で初鰹を買う場面。鰹売りが、えらのあたりに包丁を入
れると頭が落ち、腹に刃を入れると半身に分かれ、鮮や
かな手捌きで鰹をおろしていきます。和紙を重ねて作ら
れた銀色に光る鰹はまるで本物のように見えます。

In "Shinza, the Barber," the rascally Shinza buys
some fabulously expensive first bonito fish. The
fishmonger dresses the fish on stage, cutting at the
gills to take off the head and then splitting and
cleaning it. Even though the fish is made of many
layers of rice paper, it looks very real.

魚・白酒
Fish / Sweet White Sake

天秤棒で桶を担いで魚屋や白酒屋
が登場する場面があります。客席
からよく見えなくても、魚屋の桶
の上には魚が、白酒屋の桶には湯
飲み茶碗が入っています。江戸時
代のいろいろな商売を垣間見られ
るのは楽しいものです。

Kabuki gives us a glimpse of
the vanished world of street
peddlers. Even if it is not visi-
ble from the audience, there is
fish in the fishmonger's bucket
and cups on top of the keg for
white *sake*.

年中行事
Seasonal Ceremonies

歌舞伎には季節を感じさせる演目がたくさんあります。衣裳だけでなく舞台が花いっぱいになることも、小道具に季節感いっぱいということもあります。また古きよき年中行事の様子も楽しむことができます。

The feeling of different seasons is an important part of traditional culture and kabuki expresses the feeling of the seasons in all kinds of ways. There are motifs on costumes and the stage is often full of flowers. But the seasons are also expressed by showing ceremonies connected with particular seasons.

『妹背山婦女庭訓』〈吉野川〉雛鳥（中村魁春）／定高（坂田藤十郎）
Imoseyama Onna Teikin <Yoshinogawa>, Hinadori (Nakamura Kaishun)/Sadaka (Sakata Tojuro)

ひなまつり
The Doll's Festival

『妹背山婦女庭訓』〈吉野川〉では、舞台中央に川が流れ、桜が満開、部屋には見事なひな壇が飾られています。女の子の成長を祈るひなまつり。それは華やかで暮らしい見応えのある舞台です。半琴やミニサイズの大名籠なども一つひとつが素晴らしい道具です。

The "*Yoshinogawa*" scene of "*Imoseyama*," shows the doll's festival and the display praying for the health and happiness for girls. It includes miniature versions of all the things in an aristocratic court.

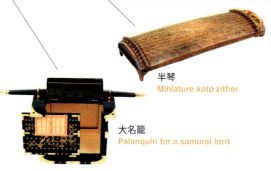

半琴
Miniature *koto* zither

大名籠
Palanquin for a samurai lord

『双蝶々曲輪日記』〈引窓〉女房お早（片岡孝太郎）
Futatsu Chocho Kuruwa Nikki <Hikimado>, Ohaya (Kataoka Takataro)

月見　Viewing the Autumn Moon

『双蝶々曲輪日記』〈引窓〉では、手ぬぐいを姉さんかぶりにした新妻が十五夜のお供え
をするところから芝居が始まります。秋の収穫に感謝して、縁側など美しい月を眺めら
れる場所で三方に月見団子や里芋などのお供え物とすすきを飾って、家族で月を楽しむ
のが十五夜。忙しい日々にふと、そんなゆったりした秋の時間を思い出させてくれます。

The play "*Hikimado* (The Skylight)" begins with a new bride putting out decorations for *Jugoya*, the fifteenth night, the night of the full moon in the lunar calendar. Strands of pampas grass are presented with spheres that suggest the moon – dumplings or boiled yams. This celebrates a good harvest and gives the play a feeling of autumn.

65

十手・刀 (じって・刀)

Jitte and Swords

家宝の名刀が悪人に盗まれたり紛失したりと、歌舞伎には名刀が物語の鍵となって登場する演目がたくさんあります。刀は役者の身体の大きさに合わせた鞘の長さ、鍔や提緒といった細部まで考慮された小道具です。また、役者がその役の気持ちになるようにと、刀と十手は本物を使うこともあるそうです。

In many kabuki plays a precious sword is the key to the existence of a samurai clan. Although the blade itself is usually a lightweight, blunted replica, great care is expended on the way a sword looks, from fitting the length to an actor's height to the fittings of the sword. On occasion, real swords might be used as well.

十手　*Jitte*

十手の中にも鉄身でできた重いものがあり、役者さんによって重さのたっぷりあるものを選ぶことがあるそうです。『双蝶々曲輪日記』〈引窓〉の十次兵衛は、十手を口にくわえるので軽くできています。

Jitte are the short batons used by law officers. They are actually very effective and on occasion the little hook can even be used to snap a sword in two. *Jitte* for star actors are sometimes hefty and impressive, but in "*Hikimado*," Jujibe has to hold the *jitte* in his mouth, so it is relatively light.

『梶原平三誉石切』の見どころのひとつ、梶原平三が刀の目きき、鑑定をする場面。ここは本物の日本刀を使っているそうです。もちろん銃刀法に基づいて扱われます。

In the key sword examination scene of "*Ishikiri Kajiwara*," apparently a real sword is used and not a prop, but it must be handled according to the strict laws regulating blades and firearms.

『梶原平三誉石切』梶原平三（中村吉右衛門）
Kajiwara Heizo Homare no Ishikiri, Kajiwara Heizo (Nakamura Kichiemon)

吹雪

Fubuki (paper snow and flower petals)

桜
Cherry Petals

洋紙を桜色に染めて、花びらの形に型抜きされています。一枚一枚見ると、とても優しい色です。紫色に染められた花びらは、かきつばた。

Cherry petals are made of regular paper dyed pink. Each petal has a very delicate color. Purple petals are for iris blossoms.

雪　Snow

四角に切った紙をネットに入れて降らせます。四角いとクルクルよく舞うのだそうです。舞台に降るだけでなく、役者さんの肩にもちゃんと雪がかかっていて、動いたときに雪がはらりと落ちる細かい演出なども素敵です。

The paper is cut into squares so they twirl as they fall. They fall on the actors' costumes as well and can be brushed off just like real snow.

手もかじかむような冬の芝居なのに、顔に汗をかいては台無しです。でも、実際は冬の場面を冬にやるとは限りません。例えば『恋飛脚大和往来』〈新口村〉の出の前には、氷を手に握って寒さを肌に感じてから出ます。

If you do a play set in freezing winter, but its summer and sweat runs down your face, it ruins the effect. In "*Ninokuchi* Village," before my entrance, I hold some ice in my hands so I can give a physical feeling of cold.

 染コメ!! Somegoro's Comment

自然を表現する歌舞伎の技術は本当に素晴らしく、紙で作られた雪や桜はハラハラと降ることもあれば、舞台だけでなく客席までたっぷり降らせてくれることもあって、とても幻想的で夢見心地になれる舞台効果です。雪も桜も悲しく切ないシーンで使われることが多く、役の悲しみの深さを視覚的に訴えてきます。どっさり降る吹雪は大道具さんの担当、舞台にある木からほんの少しハラハラと落ちる雪や桜は、小道具さんの担当なのだそうです。

Kabuki has all kinds of wonderful ways to show natural phenomena. When paper snow or flower petals fall on the stage, sometimes they fall on the audience as well: paper snow and petals create a fantastic, dream-like atmosphere. Often snow and cherry petals are used in very sad scenes; the beauty of the landscape emphasizes the pathos of the action. The snow and petals that scatter from above are done by the set crew, but small piles of snow that interact with the actors are handled by the prop people.

Ogi (fans) 扇

さりげなく芝居に花を添えるなど、目立たないけれど欠かせない道具の扇。また、歌舞伎には素敵な舞踊劇がたくさんあり、舞扇の美しさにも注目してほしいと思います。

Unobtrusively, fans are indispensible props in almost every kabuki play. And of course, they are the most important props in kabuki dance. The pictures and patterns relate to the theme of the dance and are moved to suggest all kinds of things.

中啓　*Chukei*

『京鹿子娘道成寺』で使われる、片面にお幕柄、もう一方の面に一輪牡丹の中啓。中啓とは畳んでも先が啓いている扇。

A *chukei* is a fan that spreads out when closed. This is the *chukei* used in "*Musume Dojoji*" with the curtained enclosure for Gagaku on one side and a peony on the other.

幇間（たいこもち）の扇
The fan for a *taiko mochi* (male entertainer in the pleasure quarters)

裃用
Fans with *kamishimo*

裃を着たときや口上のときに使う扇。

These are the fans worn with *kamishimo* ceremonial dress or in making *kojo* (stage announcements).

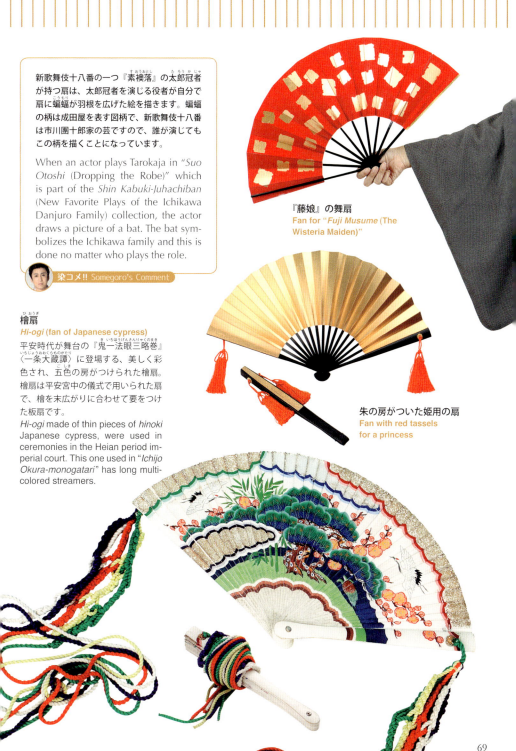

新歌舞伎十八番の一つ『素襖落』の太郎冠者が持つ扇は、太郎冠者を演じる役者が自分で扇に蝙蝠が羽根を広げた絵を描きます。蝙蝠の柄は成田屋を表す図柄で、新歌舞伎十八番は市川團十郎家の芸ですので、誰が演じてもこの柄を描くことになっています。

When an actor plays Tarokaja in "*Suo Otoshi* (Dropping the Robe)" which is part of the *Shin Kabuki-Juhachiban* (New Favorite Plays of the Ichikawa Danjuro Family) collection, the actor draws a picture of a bat. The bat symbolizes the Ichikawa family and this is done no matter who plays the role.

染コメ!! Somegoro's Comment

『藤娘』の舞扇
Fan for "*Fuji Musume* (The Wisteria Maiden)"

檜扇
Hi-ogi (fan of Japanese cypress)

平安時代が舞台の『鬼一法眼三略巻』〈一条大蔵譚〉に登場する、美しく彩色され、五色の房がつけられた檜扇。檜扇は平安宮中の儀式で用いられた扇で、檜を末広がりに合わせて要をつけた板扇です。

Hi-ogi made of thin pieces of *hinoki* Japanese cypress, were used in ceremonies in the Heian period imperial court. This one used in "*Ichijo Okura-monogatari*" has long multi-colored streamers.

朱の房がついた姫用の扇
Fan with red tassels for a princess

Paper Umbrellas

傘

紺と白は一般的に女物、渋茶と白は
男物の蛇の目傘。
With *janome* umbrellas, usually
blue and white is for women and
orange-brown *shibucha* ("bitter
tea") and white is for men.

歌舞伎で使われる雨傘には、蛇の目傘と番傘
があります。傘を持って花道に立つだけで、華
やかでぐっと色気を感じさせたり、雨の中、傘
をさして歩くだけで哀愁を感じさせたり、傘は
役者を引き立てる小道具です。芝居の中では、

雨や雪は黒御簾からの効果音（103ページ参照）
で表現され、観る側の想像にゆだねられます。
一本一本丁寧に作られた蛇の目傘、番傘の色、
傘の内側の竹の色も美しいので、ぜひ細かいと
ころも見ていただきたいです。

In kabuki there are two types of umbrellas: *janome gasa* ("snake eye umbrella") and *bangasa*
("heavy-paper umbrella"). They accentuate the presence of the actor: just standing on the
hanamichi runway with an umbrella makes him look sexy and colorful, or walking through the
rain can bring an air of sadness. The actual rain and snow is suggested by percussion patterns
(see page 103) and is left to the imagination of the audience. Every detail of these umbrellas is
finely crafted, even up to the intricate inner bamboo framework.

《髪結新三》で新三がさしている白張り傘。
This is the white umbrella used by Shinza, the barber in "*Kamiyui Shinza*."

和傘は江戸時代の頃から庶民の間で使われ始めました。竹に和紙を貼り、油をひいて作られています。蛇の目は細身で、文字どおり、丸い円形の模様が開いたときに蛇の目に見えることからその名がつきました。番傘はシンプルで素竹の良さが生きた少し太身の和傘をいいます。番傘は商家や使用人などが普段使いにしたものです。

Japanese paper umbrellas for ordinary people started to be made in the Edo period. Oiled paper is stretched onto a bamboo framework. *Janome gasa* are smaller and get the name "snake eye" from the white stripe. *Bangasa* are simpler and larger and a bit more heavy-duty. *Bangasa* were for daily use by shops and servants.

姫の外出のおともに、お付きの者が持っている日傘。少し小ぶりで上品な印象です。
This is the kind of dainty parasol held over a princess on an outing.

世話物でよく使われる骨太の番傘。有名なところでは『義経千本桜』〈渡海屋〉の銀平。《白浪五人男》〈稲瀬川〉では「志ら浪」と書かれた傘を持っています。
Bangasa are indispensible to commoner plays. The ones in "The Five Thieves" have the word "*shiranami* (white wave)" on them, meaning "thief."

履物
Footwear

おそらく芝居のために特別に作っているであろう珍しい履物や、現代ではお目にかかれない履物が見られるのも、歌舞伎の楽しいところです。履物の形や種類を見たら、その役の身分や職業がわかるものもあります。

Part of the fun of kabuki is seeing unusual footwear, ones that were always kabuki fantasies and real ones that have disappeared from real life. Often just the footwear indicates the occupation and social position of the character.

花魁の重ね草履
Kasane-Zori for a Top-Ranking Courtesan
花魁の重ね草履は、畳表をなんと13枚も重ねています。
The zori slippers for top-ranking courtesans are made of 13 layers of the coverings for tatami mats.

板草履
Ita-Zori (Wooden Slippers)
板をつなぎあわせて作った板草履。生活に窮していることを表しています。
These are slippers made of pieces of wood strung together. This indicates someone in tight economic circumstances.

男伊達下駄
Otoko Date Geta Clogs of Kiri Paulownia Wood
シンプルですが、男物でも幅が狭くて、色気のある桐の下駄。
These clogs are very simple, but even for men are narrow and chic.

吾妻下駄
Azuma-geta Clocks
芸者が履く吾妻下駄はとても粋。
These sleek clogs were worn by geisha.

いちょう歯
Icho-ba (Gingko Leaf Support)
歯がいちょうの形をした下駄。
The supports for this clog flare at the bottom,
looking a little like gingko leaves.

例えば、『加賀鳶』の道玄は歯がすり減った
汚い下駄を履いています。履物一つにも道玄
の生活感が出ています。最初から履き古した
ように見える、そんな履物にも注目してみて
ください。

Often footwear gives a clue to a character's personality and life circumstances. For example, the cheap *geta*
clogs for the masseur Dogen in "*Kaga
Tobi*" have supports that are worn
down. The clogs are prepared that way
from the very beginning.

染コメ!! Somegoro's Comment

焼桐畳付
Yaki-Kiri Tatami-Tsuki
豪快で力強い二つ歯の焼桐畳付ののめり下駄。
These clogs have a tall, powerful support of
paulownia wood charred to bring out the grain
and covered with the straw mat for *tatami*.

手ぬぐい
Tenugui (handcloths)

手ぬぐいは長方形の一枚の布。歌舞伎では、手ぬぐいはかぶりものとして使われることが多く、かぶり方だけでも数十種類もあります。現代では悪人はサングラスやマスクで顔を隠しますが、江戸時代は、髷の形で身分などがわかってしまうため、手ぬぐいで顔よりまず髷を隠したのだそうです。

Tenugui are long, rectangular cloths. In kabuki, they are often used as headgear and there are dozens of different ways to wrap and tie them. They are also used for people hiding their identities like people use sunglasses today. But in the Edo period, rather than hiding one's face, apparently it was more important to hide the shape of one's topknot, which was much more distinctive and recognizable.

(左)吹き流し、(右)道行と呼ばれるかぶり方。
Left) *fuki-nagashi* (flowing style)
Right) "*michiyuki*" style

『恋飛脚大和往来』〈新口村〉梅川(片岡孝太郎)／忠兵衛(市川染五郎)
Koibikyaku Yamato Orai <Ninokuchi-mura>, Umegawa (Kataoka Takataro) / Chubei (Ichikawa Somegoro)

(左)家事をするときの姉さんかぶり
(右)新妻の手ぬぐい
Left) *Ane-san kaburi* ("sister-style") for house work
Right) style for a newly married bride

かぶったときの形が美しくあるように、鬘とのバランスも考えてかぶります。そのために手ぬぐいの長さや形を最初から調整していることもあります。

To look beautiful when wearing a *tenugui*, the balance with the wig is important. Often adjusting the length and shape of the *tenugui* itself is necessary.

染コメ!! Somegoro's Comment

「戌の春喜寿之書初　市村羽左衛門」歌川豊国(三代)画・文久元(1861)年
Actor Ichimura Uzaemon by Utagawa Toyokuni III (1861)

それぞれの役者の家の家紋や文様をモチーフにした手ぬぐいがあります。芝居で使ったり、舞踊劇で客席にまいたりすることもあります。

There are many *tenugui* with actor's crests or names or patterns associated with them. These can be used in the play and even can be tossed into the audience as souvenirs.

成田屋「かまわぬ」

Narita-ya (Ichikawa Danjuro family) pattern, "*Kamawanu* (Nothing Scares Me!)"

七代目市川團十郎が舞台でこの柄を着て人気になった「鎌」「輪」「ぬ」で「かまわぬ」柄の手ぬぐい。

This is a pattern made popular when Ichikawa Danjuro VII wore it on stage. The phrase is appropriate to *aragoto* and it is a rebus with three pictures, "*kama*" = "sickle" + "*wa*" = "circle" + the character for "*nu*."

「児雷也豪傑譚語」歌川豊国(三代)画
嘉永5(1852)年
"*Jiraiya Goketsu Monogatari*" by Utagawa Toyokuni Ⅲ(1852)

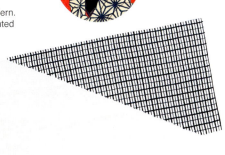

音羽屋「よきことぎく」

Otowa-ya (Onoe Kikugoro family) pattern, "*Yoki koto kiku* (Hearing of Good Fortune)"

三代目尾上菊五郎が七代目團十郎に対抗して作った「斧」「琴」「菊」で「よきことぎく」柄の手ぬぐい。

To compete with Danjuro VII, Kikugoro III created this pattern. "*Yoki* (good)" = "ax" + "*koto* (thing)" = *koto* zither (represented by a *koto* bridge) + "*kiku* (to hear)" = "chrysanthemum."

楽屋手ぬぐい

Gakuya (dressing room) *tenugui*

役者が稽古のときに使用する楽屋手ぬぐい。市川染五郎さんの高麗屋格子。

Actors use these *tenugui* in rehearsal, where they stand in for a variety of props. This one has the Koraiya check of Ichikawa Somegoro.

のれん

昔から日本では、部屋のしきりや日よけ、目隠し、また商店の入り口に営業中を示すために、のれんをかけます。歌舞伎舞台でも、田舎の家、茶屋、床屋や小間物屋の店先、神社の前の茶店などに、美しく染められたのれんが登場します。

Noren have been used from ancient times as room dividers, sunscreens and blinds. They were also used by merchants as signboards and to indicate they were open for business. In kabuki there are all kinds of pretty *noren* in country houses, tea houses, barber shops, accessory stalls and tea stalls by Shinto shrines.

段鹿子
Dan-Kanoko (dappled stripes)

『仮名手本忠臣蔵』〈七段目〉や『恋飛脚大和往来』〈封印切〉など、花街のお茶屋にかかっているのれんは絞り染めで、華やかで艶っぽい雰囲気です。

Scenes in the pleasure quarters get a bright, colorful atmosphere from this *noren* with a striped *shibori-zome* dappled design.

早蕨
Sawarabi (Mountain grasses)

田舎の家で見かけるのれん。早春、くるりと愛らしい新芽を出すことから早蕨は生命力を象徴しますが、歌舞伎ではなぜか、このののれんがかかるときは切腹の場面が多いです。

In kabuki, rustic country houses have this *noren* with a pattern of young fiddlehead grasses. For some reason, many of these scenes lead to tragic ritual suicides.

檜垣茶屋ののれん
Noren for the *Higaki* Teahouse

『鬼一法眼三略巻』〈一条大蔵譚〉の檜垣茶屋は、お能などの上演時だけ出る茶屋。鹿子文様がかわいらしい。

This is the *noren* for a teahouse that only operates when there are performances of Noh. It has a lovely dappled design.

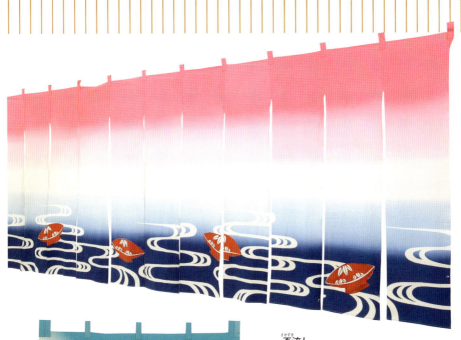

盃流し
Floating Cups
『伊勢音頭恋寝刃』〈油屋〉ののれんは、水面
に流れていく盃の文様が美しい。
This *noren* for "*Ise Ondo*" depicts a game
with cups of *sake* floating down a stream.

楊枝屋ののれん
Noren for an accessory stall
『東海道四谷怪談』〈浅草観音額堂〉でお岩の妹、
お袖が働く楊枝屋ののれん。今でいう歯ブラシ
の房楊枝や爪楊枝を売っている店。
In "*Tokaido Yotsuya Kaidan*," there is a *yoji*
accessory stall. They sell *yoji* (toothpicks),
but also toothbrushes and combs.

楽器
Musical Instruments

歌舞伎は語りや唄、演奏なども、ほとんどライブです。中でも役者さんがお芝居の中で楽器を演奏する演目があります。役者さんは小さい頃から踊りはもちろん、三味線、鼓、長唄などひととおりのお稽古をされていますが、こうした役は誰にでもできるものではなく、演じる機会も少なく貴重です。

演奏しないときは小道具さんが楽器を用意しますが、実際に音を出すときは和楽器専門店から借りたり、役者さん自身の楽器を使ったりするそうです。

Almost all the music is live in kabuki, but there are also a few special roles where the actors sing and play themselves. Even though from a young age, kabuki actors study dance and some kind of music, these roles require such a high level of musical skills that only a few actors can perform them and opportunities to present them on stage are very rare.

Instruments that are not played are props, but when actors must actually play instruments, they are either rented or the actors own instruments.

鼓・太鼓
Tsuzumi (hand drum)
Taiko (stick drum)

『昔語黄鳥墳』《うぐいす塚》物乞い・佐々木源之助は、鼓と太鼓の名手。鼓と太鼓を演奏することで卑しい生まれではなく、実は親の仇を探す武士だったことがわかります。

In the play "*Uguisu Zuka*," a beggar named Sasaki Gennosuke is unusually skilled at playing the *tsuzumi* and *taiko*. His musical skill hints at the fact that he is a samurai who has disguised himself as a beggar in order to avenge the death of his father.

『昔語黄鳥墳』佐々木源之助（市川染五郎）
Mukashi Gatari Uguisu Zuka, Sasaki Gennosuke (Ichikawa Somegoro).

この作品は、武士のたしなみの太鼓や鼓が演奏できるかどうか試されることから、「男版阿古屋」（阿古屋は右ページ参照）といわれています。

Because Gennosuke must play these percussion instruments as a test of his samurai status, this play is often called an "*Akoya*"(see right) for men.

染コメ!! Somegoro's Comment

三味線
The Three-Stringed *Shamisen*

『奥州安達原』の袖萩は、三味線を弾いて道
行く人にお金を頂戴する盲目の女乞食。勘当
された親元に許しを請いに行ったが、会って
くれないので戸口で三味線を弾きます。

In "*Oshu Adachi ga Hara*," Sodehagi is a
blind musician asking for pity from her
aristocratic parents by singing her story
sitting in the cold outside the gate.

琴、胡弓、三味線
The *Koto* (zither), bowed *kokyu* and *shamisen*

『壇浦兜軍記』《阿古屋》は、嘘発見器の代わり
に楽器を演奏させ、その音の揺れで詮議すると
いう、珍しいお話。遊女・阿古屋の美しさもさ
ることながら、琴、胡弓、三味線の三曲を聴け
る特別な演目です。

In "*Akoya*," a courtesan is forced to play
three instruments as a kind of lie detector,
with the idea that a lie will disrupt the music.
This rare play requires an actor who is
beautiful and a consummate musician.

『奥州安達原』〈袖萩祭文〉袖萩（市川猿之助）
Oshu Adachi ga Hara <Sodehagi Saimon>, Sodehagi (Ichikawa Ennosuke)

『壇浦兜軍記』阿古屋（坂東玉三郎）
Dan no Ura Kabuto Gunki, Akoya (Bando Tamasaburo)

文房具
Stationary Items

小道具としての手紙は絹を使ったり、裏打ちをしたり、踊りでは紗のような素材を使ったりと、常に客席から美しく見えるよう気配りされています。手紙を入れる文箱、筆や墨などを入れておく筆箱、そして矢立と呼ばれる携帯用筆箱など、いろいろな道具が登場します。

Various written materials and writing implements are props in kabuki, all beautifully suited to their purpose. A long, rolled-up letter might be written on silk backed with paper, or for a dance, it might be a sheer cloth. There are lacquered boxes for letters, boxes with brush and ink or even portable writing brushes called *yatate*.

天紅の手紙　*Ten-beni* ("red at top") letter

遊女の巻紙は天紅といって、上のほうを紅色で染めてあり、恋しい人を想う気持ちや色気を表現しているのだそうです。この手紙は『雨の五郎』で登場します。

A courtesan's letter has a line of red on top, as though red with rouge. It suggests her love and erotic allure. This letter from a courtesan is used, for example, in "Ame no Goro."

扇矢立　*Ogi Yatate* (traveling brush shaped like a fan)

携帯用筆箱・矢立を帯にさして、さっと筆を出す姿はとてもスマートです。

A *yatate* is a portable brush with ink and can be carried hanging from your *obi*. How handsome to be able to just whip out your brush and write anywhere!

文箱
Fubako (letter box)

実際に役者が舞台上で手紙を書く芝居もありますが、多くは前もって書いてあります。手紙のみならず、舞台に登場する上意書、証文、短冊、提灯など、あらゆる書き物は狂言作者さん*が書いてくれています。

Sometimes an actor actually has to write a letter on stage but usually it is prepared by the prop staff, written beautifully in the appropriate style. This is true of all the many written things on stage: official proclamations, contracts, bills, poetry cards and paper lanterns.

 染コメ!! Somegoro's Comment

＊狂言作者：歌舞伎の裏方。台本の整理・改訂、舞台進行（柝を打つ）、プロンプター、附帳の作成を担当。小道具の書き文字など書き物も受け持つ。

Kyogen sakusha means "playwright," but his function is closer to stage manager. He is in charge of preparing the script and running things on stage by signaling with the ki wooden clappers. He is draws up the tsukecho for the various stage staff groups and does the calligraphy for any props where it is needed.

髪結道具

油つぼ
Abura tsubo (pot for wax)

『梅雨小袖昔八丈』《髪結新三》の新三は
髪結道具を持って、商家など得意先を回る
出張営業「廻り髪結」でした。こちらは実
際に舞台で使う髪結道具。髪結の仕事は
月代剃り、顔剃り、耳掃除、髷の結い直し
など。基本的に男性は毎日のように髪結に
手入れをしてもらうのが一般的でした。

In "Shinza, the Barber," Shinza is
a door-to-door barber that makes his
rounds carrying this box of tools. This is
the prop that is actually used on stage.
These barbers would come by daily to
shave men's beards and the tops of their
heads (*saka yaki*), clean their ears and
dress their topknots.

髪結道具箱
Box of hairdressing tools
櫛、はさみ、かみそり、鬢水
入れなどを入れた道具箱。
Drawers with combs, scis-
sors, razors and a bowl for
water.

元結
Mottoi (cords to
tie topknots)

さき紙（茶半紙）
Saki-gami (paper to tie end of
topknots) (*cha-hanshi* "brown
paper")

鬢つけ油
Bin-tsuke abura (hairdressing wax)

動
物

Animals

歌舞伎には、たくさんの動物が登場します。ぬいぐるみのようなもの、しかけのあるもの、人間等身大の着ぐるみ、差し金という黒い棒が先についたもの、ホンモノにも見える技ありのものまで、愛嬌のある動物たちばかりです。

All kinds of animals appear in kabuki. There are stuffed animals and mechanical devices, there are human-sized suits, little ones operated with *sashigane* rods, and ones that look just like a living creature.

竜
Dragon
『鳴神』に登場する竜。竜をつり下げる糸は水色で「水糸」と呼び、背景が滝なので、見えないように工夫されています。
In "*Narukami*," this dragon goes up a waterfall when released. The blue string that operates it is almost invisible against the blue of the waterfall.

蝦蟇 (toad)
Gama (toad)
『児雷也豪傑譚話』に登場する蝦蟇が有名。中に人が入ってまばたきしたり、口をあけたりもできます。大きいので、動くのも大変。でも、愛嬌があるお顔です。
One famous toad appears in "*Jiraiya*." There is a person inside and the eyes blink and the mouth opens and shuts. It's very large, so it's hard to move, but it's very cute.

『矢の根』曽我五郎時致（市川男女蔵）
Yanone, Soga no Goro Tokimune (Ichikawa Omezo)

馬　*Uma* (horse)

まるでホンモノかと見間違うほど、馬らしい動き。2人の人間が前足と後ろ
足を担当し、胴体をかぶって、しかも人間1人を乗せて動くとは……もう名
人芸です。もちろん、馬になれる人は限られているのだそうです。小道具と
しては制作に2か月を要するそうです。

A kabuki horse is life size and moves like the real thing. It requires two
strong and skilled actors, one for the front legs and one for the back legs
carrying a framework for the body of the horse. Moreover, often they
must support an actor on the back of the horse. Of course, there are not
very many actors capable of becoming the legs for a horse. This prop
requires two months to make.

雀　*Suzume* (sparrows)

『伽羅先代萩』〈御殿〉で、外から飛んでくる雀。蝶や鳥など小道具をあやつるために用いる黒い棒・差し金を黒衣が操ります。

In "*Meiboku Sendai Hagi*," Masaoka uses the sparrows that fly in from outside to test the rice for poison. Often stage assistants manipulate butterflies and birds with these black *sashigane* poles.

差し金
Sashigane

猪
Inoshishi (wild boar)

『仮名手本忠臣蔵』〈五段目〉で、花道を駆け抜け逃げていく猪。前足は作り物、後ろ足は人間の足で、中腰で走るとは、すごいです。

In the fifth act of "*Chushingura*," a wild boar comes running down the *hanamichi*, goes across the stage and exits. The front legs are props, but an actor must crouch over and run and his own legs are the back legs of the boar.

鼠
Nezumi (mice and rats)

『祇園祭礼信仰記』《金閣寺》で木に縛りつけられた雪姫は桜の花びらを集めて足で鼠を描きます。その絵から飛び出す鼠は、黒衣が差し金を使って動かします。

In "The Golden Pavilion," Princess Yuki is tied up and gets free when she draws a mouse with her feet in the fallen cherry petals. The image comes to life and two mice chew her ropes away. The mice are manipulated by stage assistants holding the *sashigane* rods.

狐　　*Kitsune* (fox)

『本朝廿四孝』〈奥庭〉に登場する狐は黒衣が扱います。後ろ足で頭をかいたり、口をぱくぱくしたり、かわいい動きを見せてくれます。

In the "Inner Garden" scene of "*Honcho Nijushiko*," a magical fox appears. This puppet has all kind of cute movements. He scratches his head with his back legs and can open and close his mouth.

虎　　*Tora* (tiger)

『国性爺合戦』の猛虎退治の場面で、和藤内と虎は闘います。虎は人間が入った着ぐるみですが、その重さにびっくり。動きやすくするための工夫が着ぐるみの中には施されています。

In "The Battles of Coxinga," the hero Watonai wrestles a tiger. This tiger suit has an actor inside, but it is very heavy. There are all kinds of tricks and devices to make it easy to move despite the weight.

キセル
Kiseru (tobacco pipes)

現代では、もうキセルそのものを見かけることがほとんどないので、キセルを使って煙草を吸うという動きがとても新鮮です。また、役柄によってキセルや煙草入れの大きさも種類も違います。

Today since you don't see old fashioned *kiseru* pipes any more, its very fresh to see them on the kabuki stage. All the movements and the accessories are different with different role types.

花魁の煙草盆
Tobacco tray for an *oiran* top-ranking courtesan
塗りの豪華な煙草盆に銀のべの長キセル。
The tobacco tray is of decorated lacquer and there is a long, silver pipe.

男性の叺煙草入れ
A man's pouch for loose tobacco
一般的な男性の煙草入れ。
This is the most widely used type of tobacco pouch for men.

おかみさんのキセル入れ
Pipe holder for a merchant's wife
筒差しタイプの女性用キセル入れ。帯に差して煙草入れ部分を提げて。
The pouch hangs on a woman's *obi* with a tube for the pipe and a separate pouch for the tobacco.

煙草盆
Tobacco tray
一般的な煙草盆と銀のキセル。煙草入れには刻み煙草が。
A tobacco tray and a silver pipe. In the tobacco pouch there is loose shredded tobacco.

劇中、その役が日常の動作として、キセルを使って煙草を吸う姿を見せながら、同時に芝居もするのはとても難しいことです。1回刻み煙草を詰めてキセルを吸うと、たった二口半。長持ちするように、刻み煙草は少し湿らせておきます。

On stage, it is difficult to make a pipe look natural and act at the same time. And with real tobacco, one time is only enough for about two and a half puffs, so I moisten the tobacco a little, to make it last longer.

染コメ!! Somegoro's Comment

小道具を使った演じ分け
Using the Props Differently for Different Role Types

役者はキセルの持ち方、視線、顔の表情、指の使い方、身のこなしまで演じ分けます。ここでは市川染五郎さんに同じ着物で、キセルを持って演じ分けていただきました。

The way an actor holds a pipe, where he looks, the expression on his face, the movements of his fingers – all his movements – are different depending on the role type and individual personality of the character. Ichikawa Somegoro will demonstrate how just using the pipe differently can create different characters without changing costume.

花魁
An *Oiran* Top-Ranking Courtesan

花魁らしい豪華な銀の長キセルを使って、役者は女性の柔らかさに加え、ゆったりと大きい貫禄を動きで表現します。

A kabuki actor has to simultaneously express the softness and gentleness of a woman with the spirit and presence of a top-ranking courtesan while using this very big *kiseru*.

職人
A Craftsman

職人の場合、キセルは下から持ち、しっかり最後まで煙草を吸いきってしまう気持ちで。

A craftsman holds the pipe from below and makes sure to smoke the tobacco to the very end and not waste any of it.

芸者
A *Geisha*

芸者はお座敷では煙草を吸わず、控えの部屋で煙草を一服。男が演じるのですから、手を小さく、指が細く見えるように指を折ります。手を床につくと色っぽさが出ます。

Geisha did not smoke in the banquet room, so the only place they could smoke was a quick smoke in the changing room. A man must make his hand look small and his fingers slim. A hand on the floor makes her look alluring.

「御あつらへ三色弁慶」歌川豊国(三代)画・万延元(1860)年
Print by Utagawa Toyokuni Ⅲ (1860)

隈取（くまどり）
Kumadori Make-Up

筋隈（すじくま）
Suji-Guma
荒事のもっとも代表的な隈取。血気さかんなエネルギー、怒りや強さが感じられます。
The most representative type of *kumadori*, it expresses the power and righteous anger of an *aragoto* hero.

二本隈
Ni-hon-Guma ("two lines")
落ち着いた、芯の強さが感じられる荒事の役などに使います。
This make-up expresses quiet strength.

　隈取とは、荒事*などの様式美をより強調させるために、なくてはならない化粧法の一つ。単なる化粧ではなく、解剖学をもとに血管や筋肉の隆起を誇張して描かれています。紅は正義や勇気のヒーロー、藍や茶は邪悪、非道な敵役、茶は亡霊、魔物、妖怪などを表します。この３色をベースに50種類以上の隈取があります。隈取の色を見れば、おおよそ善人か悪人か魔物かがわかります。ここでは、わかりやすくするために市川染五郎さんにお面に隈取を描いていただきました。

　Kumadori is a style of make-up that is essential to the stylization of the *aragoto** style of acting. It's not just make-up, it almost anatomically emphasizes the swelling of muscles and blood vessels. Red represents the virtue and courage of a hero. Blue and brown are evil; brown represents monsters and non-human spirits. Using just these three colors, there are over 50 patterns of *kumadori*. Just by looking at the colors of the *kumadori* you can guess if a character is good or evil. To make it easy to understand, we've had Ichikawa Somegoro demonstrate by painting the designs for this make-up on masks.

むきみ隈
Mukimi Kuma

若々しく、色気が漂う男前。正義感の
強い役に多く使われています。
This is for a young, handsome and
virtuous character.

ざれ隈
Zare-Guma ("playful" kumadori)

滑稽でユーモアたっぷり三枚
目のざれ隈。猿のように見え
る猿隈、蟹のように見える蟹
隈などもあります。
This is the *kumadori* for
comic villains. There is one
pattern that looks like a
monkey and another that
looks like a crab.

公家隈
Kuge Kuma (court aristocrat)

藍の隈取「公家隈」は、天下を取ろ
うとする悪人、敵役。
This blue color *kumadori* is used
for villainous imperial court aris-
tocrats seeking to take over the
realm.

> 隈取は左右対称に描くのが基本です。僕は顔が小さいので、
> 筋の太さや長さを工夫して、どう描けば顔が少しでも大きく
> 見えるかをいつも考えます。
>
> *Kumadori* must be symmetrical left and right. Because
> my face is small, I experiment with the thickness and
> length of the lines to make my face look bigger.

 染コメ!! Somegoro's Comment

「東海道五十三次之内　宮　景清」
歌川豊国(三代)画・嘉永5(1852)年
"Kagekiyo" by Utagawa Toyokuni III (1852)

こ し ら え

Koshirae (preparations)

こしらえとは、出番前に外見上の役作りをすること。歌舞伎役者は小さい頃から自分で化粧をします。役者さんが化粧を始めると、楽屋の空気がピンと張りつめます。化粧のあと、役者さんと裏方さんとの息の合った連携プレーで着付け、鬘とつけていくと、みるみる華やかさが増していきます。

This is the time when a kabuki actor physically prepares for the role. All kabuki actors are trained to do their own make-up from a very early age. The moment the actor starts his make-up, the atmosphere in the dressing room becomes very concentrated. Then the actor and his assistants and the technical staff work with perfect coordination to put on the costume and wig in a very short time.

化粧道具
Make-up Set

鏡台は代々受け継がれ、道具は自分で使いやすいものを用意します。
The mirror desk is passed down for generations, but the actor assembles make-up and brushes himself.

❶ 化粧　Make-up

顔のベースに鬢付け油、水溶きの白粉を塗り、そのほか、紅や墨を使います。

After spreading *bintsuke abura* wax as foundation, he brushes and tamps on the white *oshiroi* make-up then adds red and black.

小道具　Kodogu (props)

懐紙、十手、扇子など、身に着けるものは一式まとめて準備されます。

All the props the actor will use are set out on a tray.

❷ **着付け　Kitsuke (dressing)**

衣裳さんが一式準備し、着付けます

The costumer prepares the costume, brings it to the actor's dressing room and puts it on him.

❸ **鬘　Katsura (wig)**

着付けが終わる頃に床山さんが来て鬘をかけて出来上がり。

After the costume, the *tokoyama* (wig dresser) comes and puts the wig on.

❹ **出番　Entrance**

『壇浦兜軍記』《阿古屋》の榛沢六郎の出番です。

Now the actor is ready to appear as Hanzawa Rokuro in "*Akoya*."

歌舞伎役者は楽屋にいる時点で、きれいだと言われないといけないと、先輩に教わりました。こしらえが終わったら、とにかく汗をかかないよう静かに動かずに出番を待ちます。

My elders said that even in the dressing room, people must think you must look attractive. Once preparations are complete, I wait quietly there for my entrance, so as not to sweat or disorder my costume.

染コメ!! Somegoro's Comment

黒衣 <ruby>黒<rt>くろ</rt>衣<rt>こ</rt></ruby>

Kurogo (assistants in black)

役者の演技の介添えをしたり、小道具を渡したり、片付けたり、舞台上でいろいろな仕事をする黒衣。黒衣という全身黒ずくめの衣裳を身に着けています。歌舞伎では黒は「無」を意味し、黒衣が舞台の上にいても観客からは「見えない」というお約束になっています。その身のこなしは独特です。

Kurogo are actors who assist on stage and it is also the word for the costume they wear. They pass props to the actor or take them away, and help in all kinds of ways. In kabuki, black signifies "nothing," and when they are on stage, the convention is that they are invisible to the audience. They also must move in a special way while on stage.

黒衣
***Kurogo* (black costume)**

歩き方　Way of walking
手を組むようにして中腰でささっと動く。
Hands tucked away behind or holding things so they are hidden behind them, the *kurogo* have to walk smoothly, crouched over.

小道具を渡す
How to pass props
役者さんが手を後ろにしたときに小道具を渡しますが、その小道具をそのまま前に持ってきたとき、小道具が表になるように渡さなくてはなりません。
An actor reaches behind him, as though getting something out of his kimono. The *kurogo* passes the prop to him, but it is important that when the prop is moved to the front, it is facing the proper way forward.

黒衣の大切なことは、すべてに目を配り、あらゆるアクシデントを想定しつつ、それに備えることです。

The most important thing a *kurogo* does is to watch everything and to be prepared to deal with any sort of accident on stage.

役者の後ろで隠れる
Hiding behind the actor

立ち上がる瞬間に合引を取るなど、次の仕事まで役者さんの後ろで見えないように控える。

The *kurogo* has to hide unobtrusively behind the actor so he is always ready for the next thing to do.

合引
aibiki stool

控える
***Hikaeru* (waiting position)**

立てひざをして、さっと立ち上がれる体勢で控える。
The *kurogo* waits with one knee up so that he can stand instantly whenever needed.

21歳のとき、『積恋雪関扉』で父が大伴黒主を演じた際、黒衣を着ました。その責任の重さに、稽古のときから胃が痛くなるほどでした。

When I was 21, I was the *kurogo* to my father playing Kuronushi in "*Seki no To*." The responsibility was so great it always gave me stomach aches.

浪衣
Namigo (water *kurogo*)

雪衣
Yukigo (snow *kurogo*)

浪や海の背景でつとめるときは「浪衣」、雪のシーンでは「雪衣」と呼び、背景によって黒衣の衣裳の色が変わります。
When the stage is covered with snow or waves, the *kurogo* also change their costume to match.

引き抜き

Hikinuki Fast Costume Change

歌舞伎には、観客をアッと驚かせる独特の演出方法があります。引き抜きはその一つ。帯のところで着物が上下に分かれていて、上下の着物を引き抜いて一瞬にして着物が変わるというしかけです。

There are many kabuki techniques that always make the audience gasp with surprise. One is the *hikinuki*. The top layer of the costume is divided at the waist and then cords are pulled out and the upper layer pulled off so the costume changes instantly.

引き抜き 前
Before

『京鹿子娘道成寺』は舞踊劇で途中引き抜きが行われます。後見＊は役者さんが踊っている間に、衣裳に留めてある８つの玉を抜きます。観客の目の前で変身するわけですから、役者と後見の息が合っていないとうまくいきません。霞としだれ桜の緋色の縮緬の着物が引き抜かれ、同じ柄の浅葱色の着物に変身。一瞬で変化する色のコントラストに感動します。

In the dance "*Musume Dojoji,*" as the actor dances, the *koken*＊ stage assistant pulls out cords in 8 places, then pulls off the top layer. The actor and *koken* must be perfectly together. There is a stunning change from a scarlet kimono with a pattern of mist and cherry blossoms to a light blue kimono with the identical pattern.

＊後見：通常、その役者の弟子がつとめ、主に舞踊で舞台上での着替え、小道具の受け渡しなどをする。
Koken (stage assistant): Usually a student of the actor, in dances, helps with things like onstage costume changes and handing over props.

引き抜き
後
After

ぶっかえり

Bukkaeri Fast Costume Change

着物の肩山のところから衣裳が前後に分かれて、裏側の柄が下半身まで覆うことで、まったく別の衣裳に見せるのが、ぶっかえり。ぶっかえったところで本性を現し、人格も変わります。

With a *bukkaeri*, the costume splits along the shoulders and drapes down front and back and the backside of the top layer has a totally different pattern. This technique signifies revealing the true self of the character.

ぶっかえり
前
Before

ぶっかえり
後
After

『鳴神』鳴神上人（片岡愛之助）
Narukami, Narukami Shonin (Kataoka Ainosuke)

『鳴神』の鳴神上人は雲の絶間姫にだまされた
と知って怒り狂い、白の綸子の着物から一転、
ぶっかえって衣裳は燃え盛る炎となります。
In "Narukami," a holy man is angry after
being seduced and deceived by Princess
Taema. His costume changes from elegant
rinzu figured silk, to violent flames.

ぶっかえりで衣裳の色も形も変わって、実は……と隠してい
たものをパッと見せるような気持ちよさがあります。観てい
ても演じていても、これぞ、歌舞伎！

With a *bukkaeri*, the color and shape of the costume
change instantly. This moment feels great for both the
actor and the audience, and is pure kabuki.

 染コメ‼ Somegoro's Comment

屋号と共に受け継ぐ家紋

Crests Inherited Together with Yago House Names

「鼻高幸四郎」と呼ばれた五代目松本幸四郎。
"*Hanataka* (prominent nose)" Matsumoto Koshiro V.

「ゆかん場買八郎兵衛 松本幸四郎」五渡亭国貞画・文政5(1822)年
"Matsumoto Koshiro V as Yukanba Kai no Hachirobei" by Gototei
Kunisada (1822)

歌舞伎が世界でも類いまれな演劇である理由の
ひとつは、江戸時代から現在にいたるまで、名前
を継ぎ、口伝だけでその家の芸風や得意な演目な
ども受け継がれていることです。そして、名前と
同様に役者の家には代々受け継いでいく「屋号」
と「紋」があります。役者の家の定紋や替紋の付
いた衣裳や髪飾りを身につけます。

One thing that makes kabuki rare in world
theater is that from the Edo period to the present, acting names and techniques have been
passed down from generation to generation.
Together with an acting name, an actor inher-
its a *yago* house name and family crest. Often
these crests are used as design motifs in
an actor's costumes and accessories.

1981年に初代白鸚、九代目幸四郎、七代目染五郎の3代揃って襲名しました。染五郎さんが8歳でした。2007年には染五郎さんの長男・2歳の齋ちゃんが初お目見えで、九代目幸四郎、七代目染五郎と3代揃って歌舞伎座の舞台に立ち、2009年に齋ちゃんは三代目松本金太郎を襲名しました。

In 1981, three generations of actors took names at the same time, Matsumoto Hakuo I, Matsumoto Koshiro IX and Ichikawa Somegoro VII (aged 8). Again, in 2007, three generations appeared together when Somegoro's two-year old son Itsuki had his first appearance on stage together with his father and grandfather and in 2009, he took the acting name of Matsumoto Kintaro III.

平打ちの簪　*Kanzashi* hairpins

高麗屋の家紋の入った平打ちの簪。銀の彫りがとても繊細で美しい。

These silver *hira-uchi* ("square rod") *kanzashi* hair ornaments are decorated with beautiful filigreed patterns taken from the Koraiya crests.

透かし彫り・浮線蝶
Openwork – circular design of butterflies

三ツ銀杏
Three gingko leaves

四ツ花菱びらびら付
Four flower diamonds and silver fringe

高麗屋は代々立役なので、女形の平打ちの簪を作ったのは僕が初めてです。床山さんも初めてのことで戸惑ったと思います。このページの簪は女形をやることになったときに作った高麗屋の紋・四ツ花菱、父・幸四郎の紋・浮線蝶、染五郎の紋・三ツ銀杏の平打ちです。

The actors in the Koraiya line have all specialized in male roles so I am probably the first to order these female *kanzashi* hairpins decorated with the Koraiya crests. There are the Koraiya four flower diamond crest, the Somegoro three gingko leaf crest and the three butterflies crest of my father, Koshiro.

染コメ!! Somegoro's Comment

99

個性を競う役者の文様

Highly Individual Patterns with Actors' Names

歌舞伎の中では、それぞれの屋号、または役者の名前のついた文様があります。江戸時代の歌舞伎役者は、今でいうファッションリーダー。客席を驚かせ楽しませたい一心で、役者同士が競って独自の文様やデザインを考え出し、庶民が真似して大流行しました。

There are many patterns suggesting the names of kabuki actors or their *yago* housenames. In the Edo period, kabuki actors were fashion leaders and competed to create fashions that would delight their fans. These patterns and designs were copied by ordinary people and started popular trends.

中村格子
Nakamura check

「中」に、6本の線で「む（六）」「ら」で中村と読ませています。

There are six lines ("*mu*" is another word for "six") and the characters "*naka*" and "*ra*" to spell out "Nakamura."

市村格子　Ichimura check

十二代目市村羽左衛門が考案。「太い1本線」で「いち」、「6本の線」で「む」、「ら」で市村。

This pattern was created by Ichimura Uzaemon XII (1812 – 1851). The thick line means "ichi (meaning one and the first syllable of the name)" and the six of the smaller lines can be read as "mu," plus there is the character "ra."

高麗屋格子　Koraiya check

五代目松本幸四郎が舞台でこの格子柄を着て大流行となったといわれる、太い線と細い線を組み合わせた高麗屋格子。

It is said that this pattern became popular after Matsumoto Koshiro V wore this pattern on stage. It is a plaid combining thick and thin lines.

菊五郎格子
Kikugoro check

4本と5本の合計9本線の格子に「キ」と「呂」の文字を交互に入れ「キ九五呂」と読ませた格子は、三代目尾上菊五郎が考案したといわれています。

The pattern has four and five ("*go*") lines and the character "*ki*" and the character "*ro*." Four and five are nine ("*ku*") and all together the pattern makes "Kikugoro." This pattern was said to have been created by Onoe Kikugoro III (1784 – 1849).

デザイン性の高い格子柄がたくさんありますが、線の太さ、間隔、色の組み合わせでその役の性格や立場を表現しています。

There are all kinds of creative plaid designs, but the thickness of the lines, the space between them and the color combinations suggest the actor's personality and social position.

翁格子　*Okina* check

『勧進帳』の四天王がお揃いで着ている翁格子。
This is the pattern for Yoshitsune's retainers in "*Kanjincho* (the subscription list)."

市川格子
Ichikawa check

「太い一本線」＝いち、「3本の縞」＝川で成田屋の市川格子。『勧進帳』で弁慶が着ているのも市川格子。
The pattern has one thick line (one = *ichi*) and three lines which look like the character "*kawa* (川)" meaning "river." This checkered pattern is worn by Benkei in "Kanjincho."

童子格子
Doji check

幅10cmもある大きな格子。
This is a large checkered pattern with lines 10 cm. wide.

芝翫縞
Shikan pattern

成駒屋の初代中村芝翫が、4本の線と箪笥についている取っ手の鐶をつなぎ合わせた「四鐶」を「芝翫」と読ませたデザイン。
Nakamura Shikan I (1778 – 1838) designed this pattern with four ("*shi*") lines and the pull handles for a chest of drawers ("*kan*").

黒御簾音楽
Kuro-misu Background Music

歌舞伎の音楽はほとんどライブですが、特に舞台下手、簾の奥で演奏される音楽を黒御簾音楽と呼びます。10人以上の奏者が伴奏、幕の開け閉め、役者の出入りや舞台進行を見ながら、それに合わせた音、最後の打ち出し、歌舞伎の演出効果を高めるための擬音演奏を担当します。演奏は長唄の唄方と三味線方が担当し、唄や三味線の他に大太鼓、大鼓、小鼓、締太鼓、笛といった鳴物で構成されます。この黒御簾音楽はおよそ800曲以上あるといわれています。

Most of the music in kabuki is live and in particular the music played behind the *kuro-misu* ("black grille") to the audience's left contributes to the play: setting the mood and underscoring dialogue and action. There can be over 10 musicians there, with singers and *shamisen* players in the *Nagauta* style, and flute and percussion players called "*narimono*." The basic ensemble is the *hayashi* from Noh with shoulder drum, side drum and stick drum. There are over 800 pieces in the repertory of the *kuro-misu* musicians.

三味線　*Shamisen*
長唄の伴奏に使い、3本の太さの違う弦をバチで鳴らします（79ページ参照）。
The thin-necked *Nagauta shamisen* has three strings played with a plectrum (see page 79).

大鼓・小鼓・締太鼓
Shoulder, side and stick drums.
大きさの違う鼓で、手で叩くもののほかにバチで叩くものもあります。イラストは締太鼓。
These drums all come from the classical Noh theater. This is the *shime daiko* stick drum.

本釣鐘　*Hon-Tsurigane* (bell)
時を知らせるとき、また悪役が本性を現すときなど、重要な場面転換の際に鐘を鳴らします。
Like real bells in the Edo period this indicates the time. But it also emphasizes moments, as when a villain reveals his true nature.

黒御簾から舞台を見る（国立劇場）
Looking out at the stage from the *kuromisu* (The National Theatre of Japan).

駅路　*Ekiro*

馬が登場する場面、宿場・街道など旅の場面で用いられます。

In scenes on the highway or at post stations, bells are jingled to suggest horses.

大太鼓　*Odaiko* ("big drum")

風の音、波の音、雷の音、雨の音、雪おろし、山おろしなどの自然現象、お化けや妖怪の登場など、さまざまな打ち方で表現します。

There are all kinds of patterns for this huge drum that evokes natural phenomena like wind and waves and also creates tension for eerie scenes.

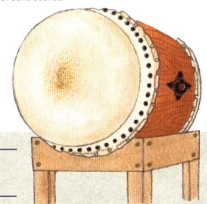

さまざまな効果音
Sound effects

自然現象や鳥の声などをそれぞれ独特な音を出す道具を使って表します。あらゆる効果音を駆使した演出方法は歌舞伎ならではのものです。

The large drum and a wide variety of instruments provide sound effects. The combination of the sound environment and the acting is an indispensible part of kabuki.

雷車　*Raisha* ("Thunder Cart")

木製の車を床で転がして、ゴロゴロゴロ…と雷の音を出します。

Pulling this wooden car across a wooden floor makes a sound like thunder.

雨団扇
Ame uchiwa ("rain fan")

団扇にビーズなどを糸で縫いつけてクルクル回すと、雨粒が落ちてくる音がします。

Beads are attached to an *uchiwa* fan to create the sound of rain.

赤貝　*Akagai* shells

２枚の貝殻をこすり合わせて、かえるの鳴き声を出します。

Two shells rubbed together make the sound of croaking frogs.

鳥笛　*Toribue* ("bird flute")

鳥の声にも使われる能管のほかに、千鳥笛、鶏笛、時鳥笛、鶯笛などさまざまな鳥の笛があります。

There are a wide variety of flutes to give the sounds of specific kinds of birds.

砂利波　*Jari nami* ("gravel waves")

紙を貼った籠に砂利を入れ、籠を傾けて波の音を出します。

Gravel is put into a big paper-lined basket and when it is rocked back and forth, it produces the sound of waves.

衣裳

Isho (costumers)

衣裳さんの仕事は大きく分けて、衣裳の手配、興行中の着付けと手入れ、興行後の衣裳の手入れ・保管の3つあります。担当する役者さんの体型や体質、色柄の好み、着付け方の好みやこだわり、歌舞伎のストーリーから役柄や役の動きまで幅広く知っていないとつとまりません。

日々の公演では、演目ごとに衣裳を用意し楽屋へ持ち込み、着付けをします。出番を終えた役者さんの衣裳を脱がすお手伝いもします。終演後は白粉や汗で汚れた部分をベンジンなどで手入れし、破れたりほつれたりした部分を繕い、アイロンをかけ、次の日に備えます。興行が終わると、着物はほどき、手入れをし保管します。

The costumers have 3 main jobs: 1) selecting costumes, 2) dressing the actors and caring for the costumes during the performances and 3) repairing and storing the costumes after the performances. A costumer is assigned to a particular actor and this choice is based on physical and personal compatibility, but also taste in costumes and knowledge of kabuki.

During the performances, the costumer takes the costumes to the actor's dressing room and puts the costume on. After the costume is worn, the costumer cleans off any make-up or sweat or other stains with Benzine, mends anywhere that is needed, irons it and then puts it on the shelf to be ready for the next day's performance. After the run is over,

現在、私たちが観ている衣裳は、歴代の役者さんや衣裳さんが作り上げ、工夫し、観客に受け入れられ残ってきた素材、色、模様、形、コーディネートです。衣裳さんはそれをそのまま残し、これからも伝えていきたいと願っています。しかし、着物自体が着ることが少なくなってしまった現代では、すでに同じような染めや織りができる人もいなくなり、素材や染料も変わってきています。そんな中で決して妥協せず、本物を残していくのは相当の努力が必要です。ただ本物の衣裳を残すだけでなく、本物がわかる人材を育て伝えていくことも、衣裳さんの使命だと思っているそうです。

the costume is disassembled, repaired where needed and stored away again.

The costumes we see in kabuki today are the result of the innovations of generations of actors and costumers to surprise and delight the audience with materials, colors, patterns, designs and coordination. Today's costumers aim to try to preserve this aspect of kabuki as totally as possible. But since most people don't wear kimono now, it is difficult or impossible to find craftsmen that reproduce the exact same color or weave. Materials and dyes have changed as well. The costumers of today feel that their duty is not only to preserve the costumes of the past, but to train costumers who truly understand real kabuki costume.

（上）綿にたっぷりとベンジンを含ませ、手際よく衣裳の汚れを落とします。（右上）きれいにアイロンをかけて翌日に備えます。（右）翌月に備えて、所化（修行僧）の帯を縫っています。
(above) The costumer wipes off stains with cotton batting soaked in benzine. (above right) The costumer irons the costume and readies it for the next day's performance. (right) *Obi* for a priest is being sewn for next month.

女形の床山
Tokoyama (wig dresser) for Onnagata

歌舞伎では、女形と立役それぞれ専門の床山さんがいます。女形の「光峯床山」の床山さんは担当する役者さんが舞台に出るときは、公演前の準備から公演中の日々の鬘のかけはずし、手入れまで、すべてを担当します。

公演数か月前に演目が決まって初日の2～3週間ほど前までに、役者さんの頭合わせをして、鬘の準備に入ります。床山さんはそれぞれ長年担当している役者さんの好みを把握しているので、舞台稽古のときにはほぼ完成版です。そして初日までに微調整をします。

床山さんはただの髪結いではなく、歌舞伎の演目、演出や役の性格を把握

There are separate groups of *tokoyama* wig dressers for *onnagata* female roles and *tachiyaku* male roles and they have separate rooms. This *onnagata tokoyama* from Mitsumine Tokoyama Company takes total care of all the wigs for the actors in his care, from preparing for the performance to putting on and taking off the wig every day and maintaining and redressing the wig periodically.

A few months before the performances when the plays and casts are set, all the wigs are made for the actors. Then the *tokoyama* styles and dresses the wig. Because the *tokoyama* has long worked with a particular actor, by the time of stage rehearsals, the wig is nearly

舞台袖に控えて、いつ何時、髪がこわれてもすぐ髪が直せるようにと、床山さんは、髪を結うときに使う元結をたすきにしています。

During a performance, the *tokoyama* is always prepared to fix anything necessary. He ties his sleeves back for work using the tough *mottoi* cords used for topknots.

し、役者さんの体格や顔とのバランスをはかりながら、役者さんを舞台でより美しく見せ、かつ演じる役らしく見える鬘を作るのが仕事です。最初から乱れた髪を作ったり、衿足にくる「鬘」が自然に揺れることで色気を表現することも。役の優しい感じ、きつい感じ、落ちぶれた感じ、色っぽい感じを鬘で表現するのは手先の技術だけではない経験の世界。床山さんは必ず、舞台稽古や本公演も舞台を観ていて、そこで役者さんと役柄と鬘がぴったり合っていると感じるときが何よりの喜びなのだそうです。厳しい世界ですが、役者さん同様、その技術や経験を絶やすことなく受け継いでいる床山さんは、歌舞伎を守っていくために欠かせない存在です。

complete. Then, before opening day, fine adjustments are made so it is totally to the actor's satisfaction.

The *tokoyama* is not just a hairstylist. He must know kabuki and its techniques intimately and know the face and body of the actor so that the actor can both become the role and that it flatters the talents of that actor. Only long experience makes it possible to express whether a character is gentle or severe, fallen on hard times, sensuous; it is not just a matter of physical technique. The *tokoyama* always takes a look at how the wig looks on stage and there is no happier moment than when the wig perfectly suits the character and the actor. Being a *tokoyama* is a very tough job, but one that is indispensible in keeping kabuki alive.

髪を少しずつ分け、コテで癖を直していきます。一人の床山さんが、一人の役者さんの鬘を最初から最後まで仕上げます。
A single *tokoyama* takes sole responsibility for all of an actor's wigs. When styling the hair, first he undoes the cords, straightens the hair with a hot *koté* poker and carefully redoes the hair.

立役の床山
Tokoyama (wig dresser) for Tachiyaku

　「東京鴨治床山」は主に立役を専門とする床山さん。一見、同じに見えるちょんまげも、実は鬘の種類がとても多く、微妙な違いを把握する難しさがあるそうです。

　配役、演目が決まると、役者さんと鬘合わせをして、鬘の準備に入ります。日々、進行中のお芝居での鬘のかけはずしと手入れをやりつつ、月の後半には次の月の鬘の準備をします。それぞれ担当の役者さんの好みを把握し、その時々の要望を理解して鬘を結う点は、女形の床山さんと同じです。また、演目にもよりますが、毎月用意する鬘の数は、平均して100〜150枚。劇場がいくつも同時に開いている月は、鬘もすごい数になります。これらを20人ほどの床山

The Tokyo Kamoji Tokayama Company mostly specializes in *tachiyaku* wigs. At a glance, all the *chonmage* hairstyles for men look alike, but in fact, there is a huge number of basic forms of wig and it is very difficult to master the subtle differences.

The process of making and dressing the wigs is the same as for *onnagata tokoyama*. Once the plays and casting have been decided, the wigs are made and then the *tokoyama* begin styling and dressing the wigs. Every day they put on and take off the wigs and do regular maintenance and restyling, but towards the end of the month, the *tokoyama* must begin preparing the wigs for the following month. But the number of wigs is different. Depending on the play, they may

その時々の役者さんが理想とするイメージに少しでも近づけて役者さんに喜んでもらうことが、そのままいいお芝居につながるとおっしゃる床山さん。役者さんを知ること、お芝居を知ることが大切だから、毎日が勉強、一生勉強なのだそうです。
Tokoyama say that their greatest joy is when the wig is exactly what the actor wants that makes for a good performance. They must know the actor and the play, and there is always something more to learn.

さんが手分けして結いあげていきます。

　立役の鬘の種類はどのくらいあるのですか？という質問をすると、「はて、限りなく……」と困った顔をされる床山さん。実際、役の数だけ鬘があるといってもよいほどなのだそうです。立役の鬘の基本は150種類としても、そこから鬢、髱、髷の組み合わせがあるので数えられないわけです。この数を考えても、役と鬘の形がわかるようになるには、相当な年数がかかることは容易に想像できます。また、役者さんの好み、頭と顔、衿足の長さ、役の性根なども把握しなくてはならないので、単に種類がわかれば、というわけにはいかないのです。

have to prepare an average of 100 – 150 wigs every month. This is even more if there are several theaters performing kabuki. This work must all be done by a team of only 20 *tokoyama*.

If you ask how many types of wigs for male characters there are, the *tokoyama* will probably look troubled and say "infinite..." In fact, you could even say there are as many types of wigs as there are different roles. For example, even if there are about 150 basic types of wigs, since you combine different types of sidelocks, topknots and back bun, it becomes impossible to give a specific number. Also, actors' bodies and performances are different, so it is not a matter of set types of wigs.

髪屋
（かつら）

Katsura-ya (wig maker)

1 髪合わせで土台の形を決めて、0.3mmほどの銅版を打ち伸ばす。
A base is made by pounding copper sheets to a thickness of 0.3 mm.

2 うどん粉と黒砂糖を混ぜ込んだあまのりで和紙を銅版に貼り付ける。
Rice paper is applied with a paste of flour, black sugar and *amanori* seaweed.

3 羽二重という絹の布に髪を一筋ずつ植え込む。
Hair is applied to *habutae* silk, one strand at a time.

4 髪をつけた羽二重を、白玉を練ったもので土台に付ける。
The *habutae* is applied to the base using a thick glue of rice dumplings.

　歌舞伎の髪は、髪の土台を合わせ髪の毛をつける髪屋さんと髪を結う床山さんによって作られます。床山さんは立役と女形に分かれていますが、両方を一手に扱っている髪屋さんが「東京演劇かつら」。役者さんが芝居しやすい髪を作るためには、頭に直接触れる部分である台がとても重要です。役者さんに合わせて、役ごとに台を合わせ、1本1本の髪を植え込むという、驚くほど繊細で気の遠くなる仕事です。役者×役の数だけ土台があるというのも驚きです。そ

There are two groups of craftsmen for kabuki wigs. The *katsura-ya*, who make the metal bases that are fitted to individual actor's heads and attach the hair, and the *tokoyama* who then dress and decorate the wig with whatever accessories are necessary. Unlike *tokoyama*, the *katsura-ya* of the Tokyo Engeki Katsura Company handle both *tachiyaku* and *onnagata* wigs. For the actor to be able to perform comfortably on stage, the metal base, which goes directly onto the actors head is vital. Every aspect of making a wig

5 鬘と鬢の部分に髪を補充する。
Additional sections of hair are added for the sidelocks and the back hair.

6 はがれないように土台に裏打ちをする。
Reinforcements are added to keep the hair from coming off of the base.

7 髪を整えて仕上げて、床山さんに納める。
The hair is straightened out and the wig is sent to the *tokoyama* to be dressed.

の工程の中でも、昔からの技法が伝え守られています。

どんな役で、鬘がどんな形に結われるか頭に入っていることはもちろん、同じ役でも家の型によって鬘の微妙な違いや役者さんの好みなども把握している必要があります。役者さんも太ったりやせたりすれば、頭の大きさも多少変わるそうで、常に役者さんの顔や頭の形の変化を見逃さず、その都度、調整をするそうです。

is extremely painstaking work. Surprisingly, there have to be at least as many bases for wigs as there are roles that the actor plays. And the wigs continue to be made using traditional techniques.

Of course it is important to know the conventions for the wigs for particular roles. But in many cases, there are also subtle differences in acting family traditions or the individual preferences of a particular actor. The wig makers also must be sensitive to the actor's physical condition.

小道具

Kodogu (props)

創業144年の「藤浪小道具」さんは、歌舞伎370年のうち、3分の1もの間、小道具を提供し続けている会社。現在も歌舞伎はもちろん、テレビ、商業演劇においても、なくてはならない存在です。

まずは附帳が出て、演目と役名と役者が決まらないと何も始まらないという小道具さん。それぞれの役者さん仕様のものが多くあるからです。必要なすべてを書き出す小道具用の附帳を作り、復活狂言などでわからないときは、過去の資料を調べ準備にかかります。役者さんとの道具の打ち合わせも含め、発注するもの、新しく作るもの、倉庫から出してくるもの、修理するものなど、すべて舞台稽古当日までに揃えます。

大道具、小道具、衣裳、床山という仕事の分担の中で、どこからどこまでが小道具さんの担当か、モノの大きさで考えがちですが、舞台上

Founded 144 years ago, the Fujinami Prop Company has been providing props for a third of the 370 year history of kabuki. Even today, it is essential not only for kabuki, but for TV and commercial theater.

Nothing can happen until the *tsukecho* notebook is received with the plays and roles and the actors cast. Then the prop crew make their own *tsukecho* for the props, listing everything that will be needed. For a play being done for the first time in a long time, they consult prop *tsukecho* for similar productions. They consult the actor on what he wants, and assemble all the props by the time of the stage rehearsal. This includes props that must be ordered, props that are freshly made, things brought out of the storehouse and things that have to be repaired.

The boundaries between what things are handled by the set crew, the prop crew, the costumers and the wig dressers are very

木、アルミ、発泡スチロール、粘土、布など素材もいろいろで、墓石、扇、仏像、小判、籠や鎧まで、あらゆるものを作ってしまう技術集団です！
The prop people have remarkable skills and use such materials as wood, foil, Styrofoam, clay and cloth to make gravestones, fans, Buddhist statues, bundles of gold coins, baskets and armor.

で、役者が手にするものはすべて小道具なのだそうです。例えば、役者が家の柱をはぎ取って立ち回りをすれば、その柱が大きくても小道具。桜の木があって、役者が枝を折って手にしたら、その枝は小道具。簪を抜いて手にしたら小道具という具合です。しかし、いちいち確認し合って準備するわけでなく、暗黙の了解で成り立っているのが、すごいところです。

difficult to understand. Most people assume that size determines whether something is a prop or not. But the fundamental rule is that anything that an actor handles on stage is a prop. For example, if an actor pulls out the pillar of a house and uses it in a fight, no matter how big that pillar is, it is still considered a prop. But remarkably, these decisions have all been made without discussion, through long custom.

附帳から芝居の準備が始まる
All Preparation Begins with the *Tsukecho*

附帳とは、上演台本をもとにどの演目のどの役を誰が演じるか詳細を書いたものです。狂言作者さん（80ページ参照）が小道具をはじめ、衣裳・鬘屋・床山に役名と役者名を書いた附帳を渡し、それぞれの裏方さんが必要なものを割り出して準備を始めます。まさに裏方さんだけが目にするものです。
The *tsukecho* is based on the script and lists the actors and what they do. The *kyogen sakusha* ("playwright" = traditional stage manager, see page 80) prepares *tsukecho* for props, costumes, wig makers and *tokoyama* wig dressers with the information they need for what must be prepared.

大道具

Odogu (stage set crew)

御殿の金襖に描かれる花の丸
These floral designs are for the gold sliding screens of a palace.

色作り　**Mixing pigments**
道具帳をもとに色を作り、色見本を作ります。
Pigments are mixed with reference to the *dogucho* and color samples are produced.

屋体の仕上げ…塗方　**Painting areas of color: *nurikata* painters**
骨組みに布や紙を貼り、塀、柱、壁、鴨居、襖などの絵を描きます。
Cloth or paper is pasted to wooden frameworks and they are painted to look like stone walls, pillars, interior walls, transoms, etc.

歌舞伎座には、「歌舞伎座舞台」という歌舞伎座専属の大道具さんがいます。唯一、年間通して歌舞伎を上演している歌舞伎座という劇場を誰よりも知りつくし、毎月の興行を裏で支えています。「歌舞伎座舞台」の前身は、江戸時代から続いた「長谷川大道具」で、その技術と知識の蓄積は、歌舞伎の大道具の歴史そのものだといわれています。

大道具は、道具帳をもとに作られます。道具帳とは、舞台装置家が描いた舞台を実寸の50分の1にした絵です。現在ある道具帳は昭和以降のもので、それ以前はすべて口承だったそう

At Kabuki-za, the stage sets are handled by the Kabuki-za Butai company. Better than anyone else, they know the only theater performing kabuki year round and support each month's production of kabuki. This company is the successor to Hasegawa Odogu, which existed since the Edo period. The store of techniques and knowledge is the very history of kabuki stage sets.

The sets are constructed by consulting a picture called a *dogucho*. This is a picture of the constructed set on stage drawn to a scale of 1/50. All the *dogucho* come from after the beginning of the Showa period. Before that, all this knowledge was transmitted orally.

There are three main sections to the set staff: *seisaku* (carpentry), *bijutsu* ("art" = *kaiga*

背景…絵かき　**Painting pictures: *ekaki* painters**
背景、自然、遠見、襖絵などを描きます。
They paint pictures of backgrounds, nature, distant
views, the designs on screens and walls.

屋体…製作　*Yatai* set unit: *seisaku*
建物などの屋体、門、塀、壁、橋など設計図を引いて、
木で骨組みを作ります。
Elements like houses, gates, exterior walls, bridges
have plans drawn and are constructed from wood.

『妹背山婦女庭訓』＜吉野川＞の道具帳
The *dogucho* for the "*Yoshino* River" scene
of "*Imoseyama Onna Teikin*."

です。
　大道具は、大きく「製作（大工）」「美術（絵
かき・塗方）」「舞台の大道具方」という部署に
分かれています。この道具帳から立体のものは
設計図が引かれ、背景の絵や色も参考にして作
られます。

「製作（大工）」は立体物などの製作、「塗方」
は立体物に色を塗り、「絵かき」は背景や襖絵
など描きます。出来上がったものを舞台で組み
立て、場面転換、解体など、実際に動かすのが「舞
台の大道具方」です。加えて、附打と幕引きも
大道具所属です。

specialists who do paintings and *nurikata* who paint areas of color), and stage staff. Plans are
drawn up based on the *dogucho* and illustrations and colors are selected according to it.
　Seisaku makes all the three-dimensional objects. The painters color them and paint any
necessary designs, like backgrounds or designs on the interior walls. The completed set is assembled on stage and moved as necessary by the stage staff, the running crew. But in addition
to handling the stage sets, members of the stage crew also play the *tsuke* clappers and pull the
curtain.

出来上がった大道具を搬入し、舞台稽古に向けて組み立て設営します。公演中も素晴らしいチームワークで、限られた時間内で各場面の舞台転換を行います。
The finished set pieces are brought into the theater and assembled in time for the stage rehearsal. During the performances, with precision teamwork, they assemble and disassemble the sets in a very limited time.

役者さんが舞台に立ったときにバランスよく、映えるものを作る。あくまでも大道具は背景。ただ道具を作る作業員ではなく、一緒に芝居を作っているという気持ちを忘れないようにしたいと常々思っているそうです。役者さんからこんな風にしたいと言われたとき、その気持ちをどれだけくみ取れるか、粋な遊び心で出された注文を同じように遊び心を持って大道具が作れるかが大切なのだそうです。だから、役者さんが舞台に立ってたくさんの拍手を受け、気持ちよく芝居をしている姿が何よりうれしいのだそうです。

The sets must always support the actors. The set crew is not there just to make set pieces, they are also a part of the team creating a kabuki play. When an actor wants things a certain way, the stage crew must be able to meet that request with knowledge and playfulness. So when the actor looks good on stage and the audience applauds happily, the stage crew is also happy to have been a crucial part of creating this performance.

附打
Tsuke uchi (*Tsuke* Operator)

附けの音は、天気や湿度などでも違ってくるそうです。
The sound of the *tsuke* can change with the weather and the humidity.

　その昔、附打は劇団や役者専属だったそうですが、現在は大道具さんの一員。走るシーンの足音、見得を切るシーンでは役者をより大きく見せるなど擬音、効果音として附けを打ちます。また、音が起こらない場面で附けを打つことを「聞かせ」といいます。同じ演目でも役者によって打ち方が違うこともあるそうです。長年の経験を持つ附打さんでも三味線や黒御簾音楽と役者さんと附打の息がぴったり合うことは年に1、2回というほど難しいのだそうです。

In the old days, a member of the theater troupe played the *tsuke* clappers. But now, a member of the set crew plays them. These are the clappers that add sound when actors are running or moving or to draw attention to something. Above all, they provide the sounds that set off a *mie* pose. Even with the same play, depending on the actor, the exact timing is different. This is so difficult that even a *tsuke uchi* with long years of experience only gets the relationship between the *tsuke*, the actor and the background music perfectly to his satisfaction a few times a year.

附打が役者によって違うように、幕の閉め方も役者によって違うことがあります。
Pulling the curtain open and shut is as different with different actors as striking the *tsuke* clappers.

幕引き
Maku hiki (Curtain Puller)

　芝居の始まりと終わり、場面切り替えで定式幕の開け閉めを専門にするのが幕引きさんです。簡単そうに見えますが、いつも同じ調子で開け閉めしているのではなく、演目によっては柝に合わせてゆっくりと開け、切迫した場面ではさっと閉め、逆にお客さんに最後の場面をたっぷり見てほしい場面ではゆっくりと閉める工夫をされています。幕切れの瞬間がお客さんにとって美しい一幅の絵として決まったところで幕を閉める……そこにも難しさと喜びがあるそうです。

Scenes begin and end when the distinctive three-colored curtain is pulled open and shut. This is also done by a member of the set crew. This is also difficult because the curtain opens and closes in different ways for different scenes. Sometimes the curtain is opened slowly with the striking of the ki clappers, then at the end of the scene, the curtain might be closed quickly. At other times, the curtain might be pulled shut slowly to allow the audience to appreciate the scene on stage.

本書に登場する演目のバイリンガルリスト
Bilingual List of Plays Mentioned in the Text

《 》は通称、〈 〉は場面を表す。　　《 》popularly known title,〈 〉act.

あ

青砥稿花紅彩画《白浪五人男》
Aoto Zoshi Hana no Nishiki-e 《*Shiranami Gonin Otoko*》
The Five Thieves
〈稲瀬川 *Inasegawa*〉‥‥‥‥‥‥‥‥ 50、71

伊勢音頭恋寝刃
Ise Ondo Koi no Netaba
The Mass Killing at Ise
〈油屋 *Abura-ya*〉‥‥‥‥‥‥‥‥ 77

妹背山婦女庭訓
Imoseyama Onna Teikin
Husband and Wife Mountains, a Moral Guide for
Women ‥‥‥‥‥‥‥‥‥‥‥‥‥‥‥ 22
〈吉野川 *Yoshinogawa*〉‥‥‥‥‥‥‥‥ 64

奥州安達原
Oshu Adachi ga Hara
The Adachi Plain in Oshu
〈袖萩祭文 *Sodehagi Saimon*〉‥‥‥‥‥ 79

お祭り
Omatsuri
The Festival ‥‥‥‥‥‥‥‥‥‥ 25、32

か

籠釣瓶花街酔醒
Kagotsurube Sato no Eizame
Jirozaemon and the Courtesan Yatsuhashi ‥‥ 18

梶原平三誉石切
Kajiwara Heizo Homare no Ishikiri
Stonecutting Kajiwara‥‥‥‥‥‥‥ 57、66

仮名手本忠臣蔵
Kanadehon Chushingura
Chushingura:The Treasury of Loyal Retainers
〈大序 Great Prologue〉‥‥‥‥‥‥ 43
〈五段目 Act V〉‥‥‥‥‥‥‥‥‥ 85
〈六段目 Act VI〉‥‥‥‥‥‥‥‥ 44
〈七段目 Act VII〉‥‥‥‥‥‥ 62、76
〈九段目 Act IX〉‥‥‥‥‥‥‥‥ 34

勧進帳
Kanjincho
The Subscription List‥‥‥‥‥‥ 36、37

鬼一法眼三略巻
Kiichi Hogen Sanryaku no Maki
Kiichi Hogen and the Scroll of Strategy Secrets
〈一条大蔵譚 *Ichijo Okura Monogatari*〉 69、76

祇園祭礼信仰記《金閣寺》
Gion Sairei Shinkoki 《*Kinkakuji*》
The Golden Pavilion ‥‥‥‥‥‥ 57、85

京鹿子娘道成寺
Kyoganoko Musume Dojoji
The Girl at Dojoji Temple ‥‥‥‥ 24、68、94、95

廓文章
Kuruwa Bunsho
Izaemon and the Courtesan Yugiri ‥‥‥‥ 35

元禄忠臣蔵
Genroku Chushingura
The History of Chushingura in the Genroku
Period ‥‥‥‥‥‥‥‥‥‥‥‥‥‥ 45

〈御浜御殿綱豊卿 *Ohama Goten Tsunatoyo Kyo*〉‥ 40、57

恋飛脚大和往来
Koibikyaku Yamato Orai
The Money Courier from Hell
〈封印切 *Fuinkiri*〉‥‥‥‥‥‥‥‥ 76
〈新口村 *Ninokuchi-mura*〉‥‥‥‥ 49、74

国性爺合戦
Kokusenya Gassen
The Battles of Coxinga‥‥‥‥‥‥‥‥ 85

さ

暫
Shibaraku
Wait a Moment!‥‥‥‥‥‥‥‥‥‥ 38

春興鏡獅子
Shunkyo Kagami Jishi
The Kagami Lion Dance ‥‥‥‥‥‥‥ 15

児雷也豪傑譚話
Jiraiya Goketsu Monogatari
Super Villain Jiraiya ‥‥‥‥‥‥‥‥ 82

新版歌祭文
Shinpan Uta Zaimon
Nozaki Village ‥‥‥‥‥‥ 14、30、31

菅原伝授手習鑑
Sugawara Denju Tenarai Kagami
Sugawara and the Secrets of Calligraphy
〈車引 *Kurumabiki*〉‥‥‥‥‥‥‥‥ 52
〈賀の祝 *Ga no Iwai*〉‥‥‥‥‥‥‥ 53

助六由縁江戸桜
Sukeroku Yukari no Edo Zakura
Sukeroku, the Hero of Edo ‥‥‥‥‥ 17、39

た・な・は

壇浦兜軍記《阿古屋》
Dan no Ura Kabuto Gunki 《*Akoya*》
The Musical Interrogation of the Courtesan Akoya
‥‥‥‥‥‥‥‥‥‥‥‥‥‥‥‥ 79、91

梅雨小袖昔八丈《髪結新三》
Tsuyu Kosode Mukashi Hachijo 《*Kamiyui Shinza*》
Shinza, the Barber ‥‥‥‥‥‥ 63、71、81

東海道四谷怪談
Tokaido Yotsuya Kaidan
The Ghosts of Yotsuya
〈浅草観音額堂 *Asakusa Kannon Gakudo*〉‥ 77
〈隠亡堀 *Onbo Bori*〉‥‥‥‥‥‥‥‥ 46

夏祭浪花鑑
Natsu Matsuri Naniwa Kagami
The Summer Festival in Osaka ‥‥‥‥‥ 55

鳴神
Narukami
Narukami, the Thunder God ‥‥‥‥ 82、96

慙紅葉汗顔見勢《伊達の十役》
Haji Momiji Ase no Kaomise 《*Date no Juyaku*》
The Ten Roles of Sendai Hagi ‥‥‥‥ 20、33

双蝶々曲輪日記
Futatsu Chocho Kuruwa Nikki
Two Butterflies in the Pleasure Quarters
〈角力場 *Sumoba*〉‥‥‥‥‥‥‥ 54、59

〈引窓 *Hikimado*〉·························· 65、66
本朝廿四孝
Honcho Nijushiko
The Japanese Twenty-Four Examples of Filial Piety
〈十種香 *Jushuko*〉···························· 41
〈奥庭 *Okuniwa*〉··························· 85

ま・や

昔語黄鳥墳《うぐいす塚》
Mukashi Gatari Uguisu Zuka 《Uguisuzuka》
The Old Tale of the Bush Warbler Mound ······ 78
伽羅先代萩
Meiboku Sendai Hagi
The Troubles in the Date Clan ················ 20
〈御殿 *Goten*〉···························· 84
〈床下 *Yukashita*〉······················· 42

矢の根
Yanone
The Arrowhead ······························ 83
雪暮夜入谷畦道《直侍》
Yuki no Yube Iriya no Azemichi 《Naozamurai》
Michitose and Naozamurai
〈入谷そば屋 *Iriya Soba-ya*〉················ 63
義経千本桜
Yoshitsune Senbonzakura
Yoshitsune and the Thousand Cherry Trees
〈渡海屋 *Tokaiya*〉·······················47、71
〈大物浦 *Daimotsu no Ura*〉················ 47
与話情浮名横櫛
Yowa Nasake Ukina no Yokogushi
Scarfaced Yosaburo ······················· 28
〈木更津海岸見染 *Kisarazu Kaigan Misome*〉··48、56

Alphabetical Index *:popularly known title

A	*Akoya**	The Musical Interrogation of the Courtesan Akoya	79、91
	Aoto Zoshi Hana no Nishiki-e	The Five Thieves	50、71
D	*Dan no Ura Kabuto Gunki*	The Musical Interrogation of the Courtesan Akoya	79、91
	*Date no Juyaku**	The Ten Roles of Sendai Hagi	20、33
F	*Futatsu Chocho Kuruwa Nikki*	Two Butterflies in the Pleasure Quarters	54、59、65、66
G	*Genroku Chushingura*	The History of Chushingura in the Genroku Period	40、45、57
	Gion Sairei Shinkoki	The Golden Pavilion	57、85
H	*Haji Momiji Ase no Kaomise*	The Ten Roles of Sendai Hagi	20、33
	Honcho Nijushiko	The Japanese Twenty-Four Examples of Filial Piety	41、85
I	*Imoseyama Onna Teikin*	Husband and Wife Mountains, a Moral Guide for Women	22、64
	Ise Ondo Koi no Netaba	The Mass Killing at Ise	77
J	*Jiraiya Goketsu Monogatari*	Super Villain Jiraiya	82
K	*Kagotsurube Sato no Eizame*	Jirozaemon and the Courtesan Yatsuhashi	18
	Kajiwara Heizo Homare no Ishikiri	Stonecutting Kajiwara	57、66
	*Kamiyui Shinza**	Shinza, the Barber	63、71、81
	Kanadehon Chushingura	Chushingura:The Treasury of Loyal Retainers	34、43、44、62、76、85
	Kanjincho	The Subscription List	36、37
	Kiichi Hogen Sanryakuki no Maki	Kiichi Hogen and the Scroll of Strategy Secrets	69、76
	*Kinkakuji**	The Golden Pavilion	57、85
	Koibikyaku Yamato Orai	The Money Courier from Hell	49、74、76
	Kokusenya Gassen	The Battles of Coxinga	85
	Kuruwa Bunsho	Izaemon and the Courtesan Yugiri	25
	Kyoganoko Musume Dojoji	The Girl at Dojoji Temple	24、68、94、95
M	*Meiboku Sendai Hagi*	The Troubles in the Date Clan	20、42、84
	Mukashi Gatari Uguisuzuka	The Old Tale of the Bush Warbler Mound	78
N	*Naozamurai**	Michitose and Naozamurai	63
	Narukami	Narukami, the Thunder God	82、96
	Natsu Matsuri Naniwa Kagami	The Summer Festival in Osaka	55
O	*Omatsuri*	The Festival	25、32
	Oshu Adachi ga Hara	The Adachi Plain in Oshu	79
S	*Shibaraku*	Wait a Moment!	38
	Shinpan Uta Zaimon	Nozaki Village	14、30、31
	*Shiranami Gonin Otoko**	The Five Thieves	50、71
	Shunkyo Kagami Jishi	The Kagami Lion Dance	15
	Sugawara Denju Tenarai Kagami	Sugawara and the Secrets of Calligraphy	52、53
	Sukeroku Yukari no Edo Zakura	Sukeroku, the Hero of Edo	17、39
T	*Tokaido Yotsuya Kaidan*	The Ghosts of Yotsuya	46、77
	Tsuyu Kosode Mukashi Hachijo	Shinza, the Barber	63、71、81
U	*Uguisuzuka**	The Old Tale of the Bush Warbler Mound	78
Y	*Yanone*	The Arrowhead	83
	Yoshitsune Senbonzakura	Yoshitsune and the Thousand Cherry Trees	47、71
	Yowa Nasake Ukina no Yokogushi	Scarfaced Yosaburo	28、48、56
	Yukino Yube Iriya no Azemichi	Michitose and Naozamurai	63

まず、歌舞伎の公演情報を得るために、歌舞伎公式総合サイトをチェックしましょう。

歌舞伎美人（日本語のサイト）
http://www.kabuki-bito.jp/
KABUKI WEB（英語のサイト）
http://www.kabuki-bito.jp/eng/top.html

公演情報を確認して、チケットを取ります。

チケットは、インターネットとスマートフォン、電話、劇場チケット売場窓口で手に入ります。また、歌舞伎座には、初めての方でも気軽に一幕から観ることができる幕見席もあります。

また、日本語がわからない方には、歌舞伎座にはセリフや解説を簡潔な英語表示するポータブルモニター・英語版字幕ガイドをレンタルすることができます。
http://www.eg-gm.jp/g_mark/portable_kabukiza.html
国立劇場には英語のイヤホンガイドがあります。

First check for information on performances of kabuki on the official kabuki site:
Kabuki Bito (in Japanese)
http://www.kabuki-bito.jp/
KABUKI WEB (in English)
http://www.kabuki-bito.jp/eng/top.html

After checking the performance information you can order tickets.

You can get tickets on the Internet or on your smart phone, by telephone or at the ticket window at the theater. At Kabuki-za there are also tickets for just part of a program, which might be good for newcomers to kabuki.

Also, for people who do not understand Japanese, at Kabuki-za there are portable subtitle receivers that translate the lines and give other explanations.
http://www.eg-gm.jp/g_mark/portable_kabukiza.html

At the National Theatre there are audio English language Earphone Guides.

チケットの買い方　How to Buy Kabuki Tickets

以下のサイトと電話では、松竹直営の劇場（歌舞伎座、新橋演舞場、大阪松竹座、南座）や日生劇場・浅草公会堂などの松竹主催・製作の公演チケットを取扱います。

You can get tickets for kabuki productions at theaters directly run by Shochiku (Kabuki-za, Shinbashi Enbujo, Osaka Shochiku-za and Minami-za) and for performances of kabuki produced by Shochiku at other theaters like Nissei Gekijo and Asakusa Kokaido.

インターネット （チケット web 松竹） **Internet** **(Ticket Web Shochiku)**	パソコン PC	http://www1.ticket-web-shochiku.com/pc/
	スマートフォン smart phone	http://www1.ticket-web-shochiku.com/sp/
	英語のサイト English	http://www1.ticket-web-shochiku.com/en/
	ユーザー登録すれば、ネット予約が可能。支払いはクレジットカードのみ。チケットの引き取りは、支払いに使ったクレジットカードを持って、劇場に設置されている自動発券機で。郵送サービス（国内のみ）もある。 If you register with this service you can buy tickets over the Internet. Payment is by credit card only. To get the ticket, take the credit card you used and there is a ticket machine in the theater that will issue the ticket. Tickets can also be sent by mail (only inside Japan).	
電話 （チケットホン松竹） **Telephone** **(Ticket phone Shochiku)**	**0570-000-489（ナビダイヤル）** **東京 03-6745-0888 ／大阪 06-6530-0333** 0570-000-489 (Navi-dial) Tokyo 03-6745-0888 / Osaka 06-6530-0333	

■窓口で直接お求めの際は右ページの各劇場にお問い合わせください。歌舞伎座では年間通して歌舞伎を上演しています。
Most theaters in Japan only perform kabuki periodically. Kabuki-za performs kabuki year-round. For more information contact the theaters directly (see list at right).

■歌舞伎座切符売場は、地下鉄・東銀座駅と直結した歌舞伎座の地下2階「木挽町広場」の一角に。一幕のみ観られる幕見席のチケット売場（当日のみ）と専用の入り口は歌舞伎座1階正面入り口左手にある。当日券の販売は朝10時から。
The box office for Kabuki-za is in the basement in the Kobikicho Hiroba marketplace which is directly connected to the Higashi Ginza subway station. There is a ticket window to the right of the main entrance and a special entrance on the left to see one section of the program (sales for these tickets are only on the day). All tickets on the day of the performance are sold from 10 AM.

歌舞伎を楽しめる劇場リスト (2016年5月現在)
Theaters Performing Kabuki Regularly (As of May 2016)

東京　Tokyo

◆ 歌舞伎座
Kabuki-za
東京都中央区銀座4-12-15
Ginza 4-12-15, Chuo-ku Tokyo, Japan
☎ 03-3545-6800
http://www.kabuki-za.co.jp/

◆ 新橋演舞場
Shinbashi Enbujo
東京都中央区銀座6-18-2
Ginza 6-18-2, Chuo-ku Tokyo, Japan
☎ 03-3541-2600
http://www.shochiku.co.jp/play/enbujyo/

◆ 国立劇場
The National Theatre of Japan
東京都千代田区隼町4-1
Hayabusa-cho 4-1, Chiyoda-ku Tokyo, Japan
☎ 03-3265-7411
国立劇場チケットセンター
National Theatre Ticket Centre
☎ 0570-07-9900
http://www.ntj.jac.go.jp/index.html

◆ 浅草公会堂
Asakusa Kokaido
東京都台東区浅草1-38-6
Asakusa 1-38-6, Taito-ku Tokyo, Japan
☎ 03-3844-7491
https://asakusa-koukaidou.net/
毎年、正月に新春浅草歌舞伎が開催される。
Every year in January, there are gala performances for the New Year's.

◆ 明治座
Meijiza Theater
東京都中央区日本橋浜町2-31-1
Nihonbashi Hamacho 2-31-1, Chuo-ku Tokyo, Japan
☎ 03-3660-3939
明治座チケットセンター
Meijiza Ticket Centre
☎ 03-3666-6666
http://www.meijiza.co.jp/

◆ 日生劇場
Nissay Theatre
東京都千代田区有楽町1-1-1
Yurakucho 1-1-1, Chiyoda-ku Tokyo, Japan
☎ 03-3503-3111
http://www.nissaytheatre.or.jp/

大阪　Osaka

◆ 大阪松竹座
Osaka Shochiku-za
大阪市中央区道頓堀1-9-19
Dotonbori 1-9-19, Chuo-ku Osaka-shi, Japan
☎ 06-6214-2211
http://www.kabuki-bito.jp/theaters/osaka/

京都　Kyoto

◆ 南座 (2016年5月現在、休館中)
Minami-za (As of May 2016, the theater is closed temporarily)
京都市東山区四条大橋東詰
Shijo Ohashi Higashi-zume, Higashiyama-ku, Kyoto-shi, Japan
☎ 075-561-1155
http://www.shochiku.co.jp/play/minamiza/

名古屋　Nagoya

◆ 御園座 (2016年5月現在、休館中。2018年再開予定)
Misono-za (As of May 2016, the theater is closed and is scheduled to reopen in 2018.)
名古屋市中区栄1-6-14
Sakae 1-6-14, Naka-ku Nagoya-shi, Japan
☎ 052-222-8222
http://www.misonoza.co.jp/

博多　Hakata

◆ 博多座
Hakata-za
福岡市博多区下川端町2-1
Shimo Kawabata-machi 2-1, Hakata-ku Fukuoka-shi, Japan
☎ 092-263-5555
（予約受付も ticket reservations at same number）
http://www.hakataza.co.jp/

香川　Kagawa

◆ 旧金毘羅大芝居 （金丸座）
Old Konpira Oshibai (Kanamaru-za)
香川県仲多度郡琴平町乙1241
Kotohira-cho Otsu 1241, Nakatado-gun, Kagawa Prefecture, Japan
☎ 0877-73-3846
http://www.konpirakabuki.jp/
日本最古の歌舞伎劇場で、毎年4月に「四国こんぴら歌舞伎大芝居」が開催される。
This is the oldest kabuki theater in Japan and features special performances of kabuki every April.

歌舞伎の舞台
Parts of the Kabuki Stage

歌舞伎の舞台は独特の構造をしています。舞台の構成をご紹介します。

Here are some of the unique features of the kabuki stage.

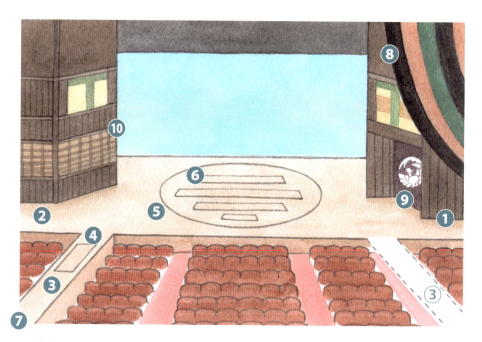

❶上手
❷下手

客席から舞台を見て右側が上手、左側が下手です。

❸花道

舞台下手から客席の間を通る通路をいいます。花道は時には城内の廊下になったり、波打ち際になったり、参道に続く道だったりと、場面によって変化します。役者は花道の七三のあたりで一旦止まり、見得を切ったり、たっぷり演技を見せたりします。演目によっては、花道と平行して上手にも仮花道（3）と呼ばれるものが設置されることがあります。

❶ *Kamite* ("upper side")
❷ *Shimote* ("lower side")

To the audience's right is the *kamite* ("upper side") and to the left is the *shimote* ("lower side").

❸ *Hanamichi* runway

The *hanamichi* runs through the auditorium on the *shimote* side. This is an extension of the acting space that can become a passageway in a castle, or water or a road. Actors often stop at the *shichi-san* ("seven-three"). That is where they strike *mie* poses and do their flashiest acting. Sometimes there is also a second, temporary *hanamichi* (3) on the other side of the theater.

❹すっぽん

花道の七三と呼ばれる場所にあるせり。ここからせり上がってくる多くは、妖術使いや妖怪、幽霊など、人間離れした存在です。

❺まわり舞台

歌舞伎の舞台中央の床は、大きく丸く切り取られ、その部分を回転させることができます。2～3場面の舞台装置を置くことができるので、場面転換がスムーズです。

❻せり

舞台の床の一部をくりぬき、その部分を上下に動かす舞台機構をいいます。大せり、小せり、花道にあるすっぽんもせりの一種です。

❼揚幕

花道の奥、役者が出入りするところを揚幕といい、通常、その劇場の紋が染め抜かれた幕がかかっています。幕には金属の輪がつけられ、開閉時には「チャリン」という音がします。

❽定式幕

定式とは、いつも使うという意味。歌舞伎の幕といえば、黒、柿色、萌黄（濃い緑）の三色の幕がおなじみですが、江戸時代はそれぞれの芝居小屋が、それぞれの幕を持っていました。現在も歌舞伎座、国立劇場は幕の色の配列が違います。この幕を開け閉めする専門職が幕引きさんです（117ページ参照）。

❾上手揚幕

花道奥にある揚幕同様、舞台上手の幕がかかっているところを上手揚幕といい、ここから役者さんが出入りします。

❿黒御簾

102ページ参照。

❹ *Suppon* lift

On the *hanamichi* at the *shichi-san*, there is a special lift called the *suppon*. Characters that make their entrance here are usually ghosts or other non-human characters.

❺ *Mawari butai* (revolving stage)

The center of the stage is cut out in a large circle and can be turned. Two or three sets can be placed on the stage at once and the stage turned to make scene changes.

❻ *Seri* (stage lift)

There are many stage lifts called "*seri*" of various sizes on the stage. The *suppon* is one of them.

❼ *Agemaku* curtain

When an actor enters or exits on the *hanamichi*, the curtain at the end is pulled open with a clatter of the curtain rings. Usually the curtain is dyed with the crest of the theater.

❽ *Joshiki maku* (kabuki pull curtain)

The word "*joshiki*" means "usual" and the distinctive kabuki curtain has stripes of black, rust colored and green. In the Edo period, each theater had its own set of colors and even today, Kabuki-za and the National Theatre have the three colors in different order (see page 117).

❾ *Kamite agemaku* curtain

There is a curtain similar to the one at the end of the *hanamichi* on the *kamite* side of the stage for entrances and exits.

❿ *Kuro-misu* ("Black grille")

see page 102

市川染五郎 Ichikawa Somegoro

歌舞伎の繊細さは
日本人を象徴しているのかもしれません

"歌舞伎の世界" いかがでしたでしょうか。

歌舞伎を分解して、一つひとつにフォーカスを当てていくことで、歌舞伎ならではの繊細な感性と、リアリズムとファンタジーのバランスが程よく調和された想像力の豊かさを感じ取っていただけたのではないでしょうか。

春夏秋冬という四季のある日本で暮らす人々は、季節の変わり目を優しく感じ、着るもの、食べるもの、見るもの、これらすべてに反映されます。歌舞伎も時代の流行だけでなく、季節の変化をも作品の大事なアイテムとして作られてきました。例えば、心おどる歓喜の気持ちを満開の桜が春風に乗る桜吹雪で表したり、ウグイスの鳴き声で春の到来を感じ、これから起こる幸福を暗示したり。この繊細さは、歌舞伎というより、歌舞伎を作り上げた役者、それを育ててきた観客、つまり歌舞伎というものを生んだ "日本人" を象徴しているのかもしれません。

歌舞伎役者は、御見物の五感を擽り、"感動" していただくために芸を深く追求し、時間をかけて試行錯誤しながら洗練していきます。ついにはそれが型となり、次代に受け継ぎ、歴史を刻んでいます。

僕の家は、曽祖父・七代目松本幸四郎から5代続き、11歳の息子も歌舞伎役者の道を歩み始めている "高麗屋" という歌舞伎の家です。伝説化され、現在も語り継がれている曽祖父の芸を、わずかに残る直筆の台本や資料を紐解くことで想像します。祖父とは僕が8歳のとき、一度だけ共演したことがありました。今も、祖父が演じているときの呼吸、舞台への情熱を思い起こします。そして、現在はそれを受け継いでいる父の背中を見て、37年目の役者人生を送っています。

皆様には、歌舞伎に長くお付き合いをいただきまして、先人を重んじて跡を継ぎ、新たな息吹を吹き込み次代へ託す、この伝承の "生き証人" となっていただければ幸いです。

歴史ある "日本らしい日本の芸能・歌舞伎" に、いろいろな距離感で、いろいろな角度から触れて感じてください。

Kabuki's attention to the finest details is like a symbol of the spirit of the Japanese people.

How did you like the world of kabuki?
By breaking kabuki into little parts and focusing on them one by one, I think you felt kabuki's delicate sensibility and its imaginative power with reality and fantasy perfectly balanced.

Japan has four distinct seasons and the Japanese people are very sensitive to the finest change of the season and respond directly with what they wear, eat and look at. Kabuki not only changes with the fashions of the day, but nature's changing seasons become an important part of kabuki. So for example, the joy of spring is expressed with paper cherry petals and the call of the *uguisu* bush warbler that foretells spring is evoked with a whistle. This depth and subtlety is not unique to kabuki; it is the product of the sensibility of the actors, together with the support of the audience, in other words, it is the sensibility of the Japanese people that has given birth to this.

Kabuki actors search for ways to tickle the senses of the audience. To move the audience, we seek to deepen our art and polish it through a long period of trial and error. Finally, sometimes these innovations become a form that can be passed on to the next generation. These little creations mark steps in the progress of kabuki.

I come from a family of kabuki actors, starting with my great-grandfather Matsumoto Koshiro VII, we have continued for five generations as the "Koraiya" group of actors and now my 11 year-old son is beginning his journey on the path of becoming a kabuki actor. The art of my great-grandfather is legendary and people still talk about him, but concretely, I can only imagine what his acting might have been like from the few scripts left in his handwriting and other documents. I only appeared in one production together with my grandfather when I was 8. But I still can remember his breath and pacing and his passion for the stage. Now I watch my father who has inherited all this and for 37 years, I have been a kabuki actor.

I hope that you will all become living witnesses to this tradition that I have been fortunate to be a part of. Over a very long span of time, while valuing the achievements of our predecessors, we breathe new life into it so we can pass it on to the next generation. I hope that in the future you will continue get to know kabuki from all kinds of distances and all kinds of angles.

君野倫子 Kimino Rinko

世界で胸を張れる歌舞伎という文化

難しいことがわからなくても歌舞伎は感性で楽しめる、そんな思いで2008年に『歌舞伎のかわいい衣裳図鑑』を、2010年に『歌舞伎のびっくり満喫図鑑』を出版しました。当時まだまだ初心者だった私のさまざまな疑問に、市川染五郎さんや裏方さんたちが丁寧に答えてくださって出来上がった本でした。この2冊を作り終えたとき、生きているうちに歌舞伎に出会えたことを心から感謝し、なんとも言葉では表現できない「満たされた」感覚を持ちました。

2冊目『歌舞伎のびっくり満喫図鑑』を出してすぐ、ちょうど6年前、アメリカに住まいを移しました。海外に出てみて、あの満たされた感覚は、世界中のどこに出ていっても胸を張れる歌舞伎という文化・芸術を持っている「誇り」のようなものだったと気づきました。どんなに技術が発達して、さまざまな舞台技術や映像などが使えるようになったとしても、人の手で伝えられてきた歴史と長い年月をかけて研ぎ澄まされてきた奥行きは、決して何者にも変わり得ないと思うのです。

とはいえ、その深さゆえ海外の方に伝えたくとも、その素晴らしさをなかなかうまく伝えられないもどかしさもあり、以来ずっと海外の方にも読んでいただける歌舞伎の本を作りたいと思い続けてきました。

そして、この度、前作に引き続き、市川染五郎さんに監修いただき、大島明・マークさんの翻訳で、念願かなって日英バイリンガルで出版できることになりました。この場をお借りして、お礼申し上げます。この本は先の2冊のエッセンスを凝縮し、初めての方にも見て楽しめて、かつ歌舞伎の奥深さも感じていただける本になっています。あらためて日本人にとっても、日本を訪れた海外の方や海外にお住まいの方にとっても、この本が歌舞伎という美しい世界への入り口となりますように。

Kabuki is a cultural form that Japanese can show with pride to the world.

I believe that when you watch kabuki, even if you don't understand much, it is always a delight for the senses. Because of this strong belief, in 2008 I wrote *"Kabuki no Kawaii Isho Zukan* (A Picture Book of Delightful Kabuki Costumes)" and in 2010 I wrote *"Kabuki no Bikkuri Mankitsu Zukan* (A Picture Guide to Full Enjoyment of the Shocks and Surprises of Kabuki)." When I started I was still a total beginner and could only put these two books together because kabuki actor Ichikawa Somegoro and the kabuki technical staff tirelessly answered my endless questions. When I finished these two books I was full of gratitude that I encountered kabuki when I had the time and energy to bring these projects to completion. I also had a great sense of fulfillment that is impossible to express in words.

Soon after I finished the second book – now six years ago – I went to live in America. Living outside of Japan, for the first time I realized that my sense of fulfillment came recognizing that this cultural art form called kabuki could stand up with pride anywhere in the world and being able to communicate this in my books. No matter how much technology progresses, no matter what new stage and film techniques might be developed, the depth created over a long history and time, and passed down from hand to hand, generation after generation has a quality that can never be replaced by anything else.

But because there is so much subtlety and depth in it, I was frustrated because I couldn't adequately explain it to people abroad. Since going to America I have burned with the wish that I could create a book that people abroad could read.

Then the opportunity to create this book came about and Ichikawa Somegoro agreed to supervise the project again and Mark Oshima agreed to be translator and my wish to make a bilingual Japanese – English book came true. I want to take the opportunity here to express my gratitude. I tried to compress the essence of my previous two books into this bilingual edition. I hope that it is a book that newcomers will enjoy, but also that it might give them even a little bit of the sense of the subtlety and depth of kabuki. I hope that this book will be an entrance into the world of kabuki, first for Japanese getting reacquainted with their own culture, and for foreigners visiting Japan, and hopefully, for people all around the world.

■協力
松竹株式会社
松竹衣裳株式会社
日本演劇衣裳株式会社
歌舞伎座舞台株式会社
藤浪小道具株式会社
東京演劇かつら株式会社
東京鴨治床山株式会社
有限会社光峯床山
公益社団法人日本俳優協会
office そめいろ
■舞台写真提供
松竹株式会社（下記以外）
国立劇場（65, 83, 96, 102ページ）

■ブックデザイン
佐久間勉・佐久間麻理（3Bears）
■撮影
野村佐紀子
（帯・プロフィール・5ページ・染コメ‼
の市川染五郎）
■浮世絵協力
垣下和之　「浮世絵ぎゃらりぃ」
http://www.ukiyo-e.jp/
■イラスト
光安知子
■校正
小学館クリエイティブ・小学館出版クォ
リティーセンター

◆本書は2008年刊『歌舞伎のかわいい衣
裳図鑑』、2010年刊『歌舞伎のびっくり満
喫図鑑』（いずれも君野倫子著・市川染
五郎監修／小社刊）を1冊にまとめて加
筆、再編集し、英訳をつけたものです。

〈上記2冊のスタッフ〉
◆アートディレクション・ブックデザイン／
山口美登利・宮巻麗・川添藍
◆撮影／寺川真嗣・武井正雄・峯岸雅昭・
五十嵐美弥・藤岡雅樹
◆編集協力／株式会社松本幸四郎事務
所・矢口由紀子

バイリンガルで楽しむ歌舞伎図鑑

2016年6月20日　初版1刷発行

著　者　君野倫子
監修者　市川染五郎
英　訳　大島明・マーク

発行者　神永　曉
発行所　株式会社小学館
　　　　〒101−8001
　　　　東京都千代田区一ツ橋2−3−1
電　話　編集　03-3230-5164
　　　　販売　03-5281-3555

印刷所　日本写真印刷株式会社
製本所　株式会社若林製本工場

制作：河合隆史・酒井かをり・斉藤陽子／販売：窪　康男／宣伝：阿部慶輔
編集：長尾純子